T0131601

How to Do Life Without the Wife

DAVID JONES

BALBOA.PRESS
A DIVISION OF HAY HOUSE

Balboa Press books may be ordered through booksellers or by contacting:

Balboa Press
A Division of Hay House
1663 Liberty Drive
Bloomington, IN 47403
www.balboapress.com
844-682-1282

Because of the dynamic nature of the Internet, any web addresses or
links contained in this book may have changed since publication and
may no longer be valid. The views expressed in this work are solely those
of the author and do not necessarily reflect the views of the publisher,
and the publisher hereby disclaims any responsibility for them.

The author of this book does not dispense medical advice or prescribe the use
of any technique as a form of treatment for physical, emotional, or medical
problems without the advice of a physician, either directly or indirectly. The
intent of the author is only to offer information of a general nature to help
you in your quest for emotional and spiritual well-being. In the event you use
any of the information in this book for yourself, which is your constitutional
right, the author and the publisher assume no responsibility for your actions.

Any people depicted in stock imagery provided by Getty Images are
models, and such images are being used for illustrative purposes only.
Certain stock imagery © Getty Images.

Print information available on the last page.

ISBN: 978-1-9822-7894-6 (sc)
ISBN: 978-1-9822-7896-0 (hc)
ISBN: 978-1-9822-7895-3 (e)

Library of Congress Control Number: 2022908837

Balboa Press rev. date: 06/20/2022

To all of those who have been a part of my life, including those who have added value in some way as well as provided me with lessons and challenges. To my ex-wife, who made the journey to this book possible. And to my life coach, Rachel Mango, who has shown guidance, encouragement, support, and most importantly, patience along this exercise of growth.

CONTENTS

Introduction: My Story ix

Chapter 1   Everything Does Not Happen for a Reason 1
Chapter 2   Making New Friends 3
Chapter 3   Taking Responsibility 25
Chapter 4   Self-Love, Loving Yourself 34
Chapter 5   Dating 43
Chapter 6   Exercise 58
Chapter 7   Self-Care 67
Chapter 8   Erectile Dysfunction 84
Chapter 9   Goals 96
Chapter 10 Budget 108
Chapter 11 Career 122
Chapter 12 Diet 132

In Closing 143
References 145
About the Author 147

INTRODUCTION

My Story

Don't judge my life if you haven't walked my journey.
—Samantha C.

After twenty-five years being with my wife, of which eighteen years were marriage, I found myself single again. I thought being free of the issues I had had in the marriage would allow me to rediscover myself, dust off those old goals, and start a new life full of joy and possibilities. After all, for the first time in a long time, I was in control of my destiny. That was my perspective of divorce; however, the next four years would prove that signing some divorce papers does not change who one is.

Divorce left me *with me*.

When I was once again alone in life and nothing changed, other than having a cold bed to crawl into, I realized that the problem might not have been the other person. It was easy to blame my spouse; I could justify it to myself, but when I made that huge leap and was single again, I needed to examine myself when nothing in fact did change.

I will admit for four years I did not realize things were not changing; I thought life was good. I was focused on starting my life over; I was focused on working, paying my bills, paying my wife's lawyer, and putting my daughter (who was a freshman) through college for the next four years. I was focused on survival, figuring out how to do a budget and live within it. I was not focused on myself; I was concerned about everything else.

It was at my daughter's college graduation, sitting next to my ex-wife, when I realized four years had gone by. I was in the same spot in my life as I was four years earlier. One thing I did do was finished college. In fact, I obtained my bachelor's degree a few months before my daughter. Other than my degree, I was in a rut.

Interestingly, sitting there next to my ex-wife, I had some time to spare as there were a thousand kids waiting to be called up on stage. I took a look at my Facebook, and one of those "Five years ago today" items popped up; it was a nice shout-out from our older daughter who was also at the graduation, sitting opposite of my wife. The shout-out was for our anniversary; it was hard to believe just five years ago we were married. Then it hit me, much to my ex's disdain, this day was our wedding anniversary; I had forgotten. It was an interesting day being our marriage anniversary and our daughter's graduation.

It was a wakeup call. When we put time into perspective, we realize how much time we have wasted thinking or talking about doing things. It reminded me of the time I built this large deck in our backyard; it was huge with different levels, an atrium, benches, and lighting. I did it all by myself and was really proud; however, a year later, it was torn down to make room for the pool.

At the time, my older daughter was in basketball camp over the summer and I remember a conversation with her teammate's mother. I told her about the deck I was building and how difficult it was. A year later, same summer basketball camp, same mom, I again told her about the deck. "You told me that last year," she said. I was shocked it had taken me over a year to finish, but it was her comment that kicked me into overdrive to finish it up.

The purpose of this book is to get you moving, to reinvent yourself as the new man you are. As mentioned, I sat around for four years just surviving. The lessons learned over the past few years have transformed me, and I'm here to share those lessons with you in an attempt to help you along your journey.

In a word, this book is about "perspective," my perspective as to what I have encountered, learned, and studied about. As of this writing, I have finished my master's in business administration and have put my toe into getting my PhD. I have a life coach who has provided me with guidance and growth, and in turn, I have also become a life coach.

There is a quote by Buddha that has motivated me over the past few years. "The trouble is, you think you have time." That quote is over my desk; it is something I tend to forget about, but when I look up and try to figure out why things aren't working, there is my answer. Time is passing by at this very moment; it will continue to. Four years from now, will we look back and wonder where the time went? Or will we have been working on ourselves being the man we want to be? The time will pass regardless. At a minimum, I ask that we start taking regular small steps, which are outlined in this book.

What is possible? Anything! I know that is cliché, but for each of us, what is possible is what we cannot possibly imagine being a reality in our life. That is different for each of us. What is "anything" to me might be lame or boring to most, but to me, it's important. And on the other side of the coin, what is "anything" for you might not appeal to others. I am going to encourage you to not just think big but do things that make you uncomfortable. Being uncomfortable will open up new opportunities and possibilities.

Being uncomfortable has been one of the biggest contributors to most of my growth. Being uncomfortable is something my life coach always challenges and encourages me to do. I am not sure whether she coined the phrase or not; however, I do give her credit for it and will therefore publish it here:

If you don't want to, you have to. (Rachel Mango)

Let me give you my example. As of this writing, I am the president at my local Toastmasters club. I have given many speeches and have done every role in the club more than once, even being the "Toastmaster of the Day" as least a dozen times. Recently I was in a speech contest, my second one. And I came in third out of three, which means I lost! It was a learning experience for becoming a better communicator.

Learning what each failure means and how to improve upon it made me grow. Yes, I lost that contest. I have been in Toastmasters for about two years now. The guy who won first has been in Toastmasters for eight years, just a point of reference. I did a self-assessment and came to the realization as to why I came in third. My material was stronger than both of the other speakers', and my delivery and approach to the contest were outside the box, which was evidently too much for the judges.

What was most important of that loss was I amazed myself!

A few years ago, when I was sitting in a Toastmaster meeting as a guest, I had a completely different view. I was scared to my core. When I started with my club, I would never have believed that I would be in a speech contest, president of the club, be the "Toastmaster of the Night" over a dozen times, or become an area director.

Before joining Toastmasters, I was the person who sat in the back of the room with my head down. I prayed the speaker would not call on me or ask me to participate. If a point came when the speaker was looking in my direction, I would pretend I was writing and taking notes. "Please don't call on me. I am writing something very important that will change the world!" I did not want to participate with anything involved with standing up and speaking to a group.

Today? Oh, I won't shut up! I have some things to say—some thoughts I've had rattling around in my head for years. A presenter who calls on me is doomed to lose control of the presentations or speech. I feel comfortable and good about getting up and speaking now.

I have come so far in my passion for public speaking that it is amazing to me. I came in third, which means the judges didn't think I did as well as the others. It didn't matter that I came in third. The judges didn't know who I was a year ago versus who I am now. I didn't want to, but I'm glad I did join.

Let's go back to "What is possible? Anything?" For me, obviously being able to get up and do a humorous speech in front of people is far beyond anything I would have ever considered. You might think it's irrelevant or something you have no interest in, but the point is you will find little things that will make you amaze yourself.

If you are like me, asking for and getting a divorce was the hardest thing I have ever done. We were together twenty-five years, married eighteen; it was very difficult for me, and at times it still is. As we deal with the difficulties of divorce, loss, or separation, we are getting stronger. We are gaining that inner strength we did not know we have.

Going forward, any challenge we come up against will not be as difficult as what we have or are currently enduring. Even if we did not want the divorce, she did, and we are now single; there are numerous obstacles we have had to overcome. Those losses, setbacks, and failures are all things to build upon. There are few things we will encounter that will be more difficult than a divorce. We came out on the other side; we are still here; we can handle anything!

Enough chitchat. Let's get to rediscovering you and becoming the person you want to become. I am going to have some fun chapters and some tough chapters. The tough chapters are the ones I hope you'll find your growth in. Maybe through my experiences and journey an idea will spark inside you and you will act and start to gain momentum in your life.

The goal of this book is for you to discover you—to live your story. You have the knowledge, experiences, and dreams to get where you want to go. I'm going to share my experiences and research to help you along your journey. I'll be your tour guide pointing out interesting things along the way so you can come to your own conclusions, awakenings, and hopefully become a new you.

Through your self-discovery as you read the following chapters, you'll find some tools you are going to like. These tools will help you create a life you're going to love.

CHAPTER 1

Everything Does Not Happen for a Reason

You are standing in the reality of your divorce or loss. You feel the pain. Don't let others tell you how to feel. During your journey you will come across many people with good intentions who want to give you advice. They may think they know what is best; however, we all have different circumstances. Our emotions and difficulties cannot be fixed with a brief conversation or words of encouragement.

Suffering is an invisible, emotion, and actual pain. You can see, live, and feel it, others cannot. You take care of you. Read a book, listen to others for advice, see a therapist, or get a coach—do what feels right. Clichés like "everything happens for a reason," "when one door shuts another one opens," and "life will turn out the way it's supposed to" are just that, clichés. They are not real advice or remedies to your pain and struggles. One quote will not fix anything.

Everything does not happen for a reason; things just happen in life, and we need to learn to deal with them. People in our

David Jones

lives mean well; be polite, listen to what they say, and put that information in the file cabinet located in the back of your mind for usage later.

Yes! That's it for this chapter. I want you to get momentum; you can now say you've completed chapter 1 of the book.

CHAPTER 2

Making New Friends

A real friend is one who walks in when
the rest of the world walks out.
—Walter Winchell

When we find ourselves single again, we tend to lose our friends. For the most part, our friends are all still married with kids. They cannot hang out with us because they have dad and husband duties to do.

In this chapter, I will discuss why we need to seek out new friendships and why, as humans, we need to have friends for our emotional well-being. I will then move to discuss what a friend is—a true friend, not a buddy we sit around with, eating pizza and watching the game. The paragraph above indicates why we need new friends; therefore, we will have a discussion of how to get friends. And no, do not go onto a dating app and change your settings to man seeking friends with other men; you will have an entirely different experience from what you are most likely looking for! Or do—you do you!

Once we form some friendships, we will need to cultivate those friendships and build a foundation to make the other person a true friend. Finally, we will explore why we need to be alone at times. Having friends is great, but we do need to be alone as well. We need to be comfortable being alone. Do not be needy. How many needy people do you enjoy hanging out with?

Where did all of my friends go?

When I was married, we used to always have company; we would have dinner parties, go out to dinner with others, and socialize regularly. A group of us would spend the day going to various vineyards or go out all night at clubs. Friends were plentiful back then. There was always something to do with the group of friends we had. Back then, we'd have to say no to some invitations just so we could have some alone time.

What happened? Netflix is my new companion! I can mix it up and check out Amazon Prime Video or Hulu, but all of my humans are gone.

Remember your friends, the ones you hung out with so many times? You, your wife, and kids went to birthday parties with them, out to dinner on double dates, and maybe even took family vacations to Disney with them. There will not be an immediate pullback; however, it will happen. There are a number of reasons this unfortunate truth can and most likely will happen.

When a married person talks with a separated or divorced friend, that person directly or indirectly learns the benefits and drawbacks of separation and could become more accustomed to or interested in the prospects. If someone's significant other has been on the fence about the viability of their relationship, a divorce within their social circle can become a turning point. According to research, if one gets divorced, there is a 147 percent greater chance of a friend's marriage coming to an end. It has been shown that even a coworker's divorce has the same effect; it increases the likelihood of divorce for work acquaintances by 55 percent. Interestingly, those with children in the marriage will likely remain married with the same scenario. Their friends can get divorced, yet it will not change the couple with the children's bond.[1]

As the good-looking, personable person you are, you become a threat to other couples now that you are single. You are appealing to the wife of an unhappy couple and your married friend can become insecure with having you around his wife. Or the kiss of death, which many comedies and movies exaggerate, is when you start dating someone new and you have that new relationship smell.

You are holding hands, kissing, and saying loving things to each other. Your flirtation and looking into each other's eyes with those smirks on your face can make your friends with their so-so or stagnant relationship want to puke. You will not be invited out as a couple again; you remind them they have a mediocre marriage that, unfortunately, they are content with. To them, your energy is not contagious; it is demoralizing.

Regardless of how the breakup or divorce played out, friends inevitably feel they have to pick a side. It can be awkward if you ask about your ex and they have to tell you, which is taking away from the privacy of your ex. If they have a party, do they invite you as well as invite your ex who is now dating someone? Are they obligated to tell you she is dating someone? It gets messy; therefore, it is easier for friends, especially a couple, to pull away from you.

If you think back to when you were married, with those who you hung out with on a regular basis, was there a single person who was always there with you? Most likely not. We tend to fall into our social groups by relationship status: singles with singles and couples with couples. You should make it easy on your couple friends if you care about them; you do not have to end it or walk away, but if they are gradually pulling away from you, then don't fight the process. Remember that divorce has consequences.

Guys who are going through a breakup or a divorce have heavy emotions and rightfully so. Unfortunately, as guys, our guy friends do not want to hear about the ex, the emotions, or the problems we are having with her. For a guy, it is difficult enough to have an emotional conversation with our own partner; we definitely do not want it with a friend. We become the Debbie Downer of the group because we are emotionally needy and guy friends do not know how to deal with it.

Divorce hurts and breaks up families and also friends.

Hanging out with our previous couple friends can hurt us emotionally. It reminds us of what we used to have—all the good times we had as a couple with those other couples. If you decide it is too difficult to spend time with these couples, you can express it to them by saying that you need a break for a little bit as the pain is enhanced every time you are with them. You have to look out for your own emotional well-being first.

Unfortunately, we lose friends because they show their true colors while we are going through separation. This happened to me. The decision to get divorced was an unexpected one; it was that final argument that set it in motion. Before that argument, everything was status quo—boring and mundane but tolerable.

We had planned and paid for a Greek cruise with one of our closest couple friends far in advance of the separation.

When the decision was made to separate, I called my friend and told him what was going on. After twenty-five years, we were going our separate ways and I was not going on the cruise. I told him I was not sure whether my ex was going or not. She did end up going with them. He responded with anger toward me—complained that I was being selfish, said that they had been looking forward to it, and said that I should just go. Really? Just go! Never mind my and my ex's emotional states or the struggles and difficulties we were going through, just go so the four of us could have fun.

This conversation happened several times over the next few months. It was a difficult decision not to go; however, I knew if I did, my ex and I would get back together. How could we not? A romantic cruise through the Greek Islands. The whole situation sucked for me and my ex who went but had a horrible time, yet our friends were angry with me.

Finally, some people feel awkward and do not know what to say to you. You shouldn't put them in a position of giving you their approval. They might not approve of your breakup or divorce based on their values or cultural or religious views. There are friends who will be disappointed you gave up or are "doing this to your children." There are any number of reasons or scenarios that will cause us to lose friends; it is part of the process and journey of life.

Overall, people have to get on with their lives. We have the right to be in pain, the right to want to sit around and do nothing. Our friends will be there for us in the beginning; however, over time, they will often shift from being a supportive friend to being a friend that has their own issues to handle each day. If you become overly needy, you will make them uncomfortable.

Eventually, you will learn to move forward with your grief, not move on from it.

Six years later, I still have moments of sadness from my divorce, yet each morning I wake up and start a new day, a new journey. We now have an understanding as to why we have lost friends. Let's talk about why we actually need friends.

Why We Need Friends

Having friends in our lives is not just having someone to hang out with, to do things with, or talk to; it's been proven friendships can extend life expectancy and lower the chances of heart disease. Friendships help us grow, assimilate, and survive in our journey through life. You see, our brains, especially the neurobiological endogenous opioid system, react in a positive way when we engage in social relationships. "In 2016, researchers found evidence of the release of oxytocin in primate brains during social interactions, and later that year, psychologists conducted a study that suggested levels of pain tolerance can predict how many friends someone has."[2]

All of the friends we have had through our lives have shaped who we are today. Based on those early childhood friends till now, they have guided us along a path whether we know it or not. Personally, I believe everything we have done in life, every encounter, every job, friend, relationship, flat tire, overheated radiator, missed flight, all things in life, have projected us to exactly where we are now. Our friends, based on their interests, have influenced our journey. If we look at it in that context, there is no good or bad; it is what it is. Our marriage, our divorce, our friends, our loss of friends—all of those things have made us who we are today.

Friends come into play when we need help with something. Most jobs we apply for need some personal references; friends fit into that category. Friends can help us get jobs by telling us of a job opening or referring us to another friend who knows of an opening. Friends can help us meet a romantic partner, either as our wing man at a bar or based on someone they know. If we have the right friends, they can encourage us in all of our endeavors and goals we seek; we will touch upon that in a little bit.

Friends also introduce us to their friends, who in turn become our friends. This increases our tribe, our gang, our group, or whatever we like to call each other; mine is a tribe. If that base friend is a quality person, chances are their friends are quality, and by association, we will be with a good group of people. Like attracts like.

Being single again, I had to adjust to isolation, which was a major contributing factor to gaining weight, drinking too much, and depression. Sitting around bored all of the time slowly ate away at me. Friends make us happy; our mood changes as we enter the arena of friends.

If you are currently sitting at home and watching TV all alone with no one to call, that is a good thing! You're a blank slate. If you are sitting around with a couple of friends and watching a ball game, having pizza and a beer, and still wearing the clothes you had on when you woke up, it might be time for some changes, and not just your outfit.

At this new phase of our life, who we surround ourselves with is important to our growth or to our lack of growth. Friends are considered our peer group. We tend to look for groups we can fit in with; we want to be a round peg in a round hole. Most people's lives are a direct reflection of their peer group. Instead of looking for pegs the same shape as us, we will want to challenge ourselves to stretch and be uncomfortable by being with those who are not our mirror image.

As single men, we might have an image of the person we want to become; the right friends and acquaintances can help us get there or drag us down. If they drag us down, we remain at the status quo. If we have higher expectations for ourselves than those we socialize with, they can become an obstacle to our growth. Not because they want to pull us down but because they do not want to lose us.

If they undermine us and our dreams, it can because they do not have our ambitions and fear being left behind. Whoever we spend time with, we become; therefore, lead and bring our current peer group up, or get a new group. There will be times where our friends are in that doom and gloom mode, yet we are happy, things are happening, and we will find ourselves stifling our emotions because we feel guilty things are going well for us and not our friends. Unfortunately, those are the friends we need to slowly let go.

I saw an interview with Snoop Dog, who said it perfectly.

> As you grow, you lose certain homies, because it's called closing the gap. This is the gap when we start (showing his hands apart). This is the gap as we grow (hands farther apart). Notice how you grow, and they don't. So how do you close the

gap? You gotta come back down (closed hands together). When you come back down you lose. So, you gotta keep going up. That's why to close the gap gotta be them, catching up to you. And if they don't catch up, you gotta leave them behind.[3]

What Is a Friend?

My definition of a friend is someone who does *not* accept us for who we are; they tell us the truth. They tell us what is going on and challenge us to be better. They don't appease us or become yes men. Our friends/peer group needs to have higher expectations, have friends that challenge us.

We tend to have friends who are similar to us; like attracts like. Our goals and priorities tend to be in line with those of our friends; they help support our goals because they are the same. Our close friends are there for us for the good and bad times. We need to be selective with our friends, those who will really matter for our well-being.[4]

Friends are the ones who are honest and give us a reality check when we need it. Friends are the ones who know us so well they can give advice—sound advice if they are a true friend. We go to them for a second opinion regarding a romantic interest or job. We'll ask, "Am I missing something, or does this seem good?" Friends have a good perspective of who we are, what makes us tick. When we need to do a personality assessment in a magazine or on a web site, who do they tell us to ask? Our friends.

Friends are the people we go to with a crazy idea and hopefully they will go along with it. We might want to clean up a park, do a protest, or help feed the homeless. We are less prone to do things like this by ourselves, but with our friends next to us, we'll do it and grow together. With those close friends, we can then hit social media and create a wave of others to join us on our journey.

We benefit from having friends; however, we also benefit from being a friend. By supporting our friends' priorities, we grow as an individual as well as build upon that relation of being a good friend to others. I've personally experienced this where I have friends who lifted me up, who encouraged me, and who challenged me. Over time, I grew and became the person to help support them, challenge, give them new experiences, and became the person they were to me.

There will be a paradigm shift; they lead me, now I lead them, and they will once again raise their standards and lead me. A friend will challenge us and give us continual growth. If our friends are not doing that, refer back to the Snoop Dog interview. You'll know what you need to do.

With our friends, we ask, "Can we be ourselves around this person, or do we need to watch what we say?" Do we feel happy when we are with these people, or are we just passing time? Are they helping us to grow? Do they challenge and encourage us? Answering these questions can help us determine whether we have real friends or not. I read the best quote about being a friend, one that I'll admit I have not lived by, but since I read it, I have started to make a change in the right direction. "Don't tell me what they said about me. Tell me why they were so comfortable to say it around you."

Someone who is a true friend will stand up for us. We in turn should be a friend that no one will gossip to about other friends in the group because we will shut them down and stand up for the other person. I'm guilty of this, but not anymore. It's not fair on so many levels. The friend we are gossiping about isn't there to defend themselves. The person we are gossiping to is put in a bad position to either offend us by pushing back or to stay silent.

Finally, by talking negatively about others, it lessens our leadership, lessens our worth. If we gossip to person A about person B, person A will wonder who we gossip to about them. Focus on the positive, find good in everyone, and don't disrespect our friends by telling them gossip about others.

Give so much time improving yourself that you have no time to criticize others.[5]

How to Get Friends

Motivational speaker Zig Ziglar said, "When we go out to seek a friend, they are hard to find, but when we go out to be a friend, they are everywhere."

Many of us struggle to meet people other than work friends or acquaintances. Finding new friends is in fact difficult; however, it is never too late or impossible. And no, Facebook friends do not count. I have found some amazing people on Facebook whom I have a good rapport with; however, we don't hang out and can't shake hands or hug, nor are they anyone I would reach out to for help to move or have dinner with. That is where actual friends come into play: the real world, real humans.

I've found a few ways to make friends that I will share with you. A couple of years ago, I was the type who kept my head down, flew under the radar, and didn't want to interact. Now I am the opposite. I won't shut up. I enjoy engaging with and chatting with people about anything. It is my friends, acquaintances, and activities that have made that change. Being around the right group will bring like-minded people into our lives. We need to go do activities, join clubs, and get outside our comfort zones to find friends.

Going to the bar or to the gym are limited ways to find friends. Are those the people we want to build friendships with, or are they simply lift-and-drink buddies? Yes, they can be both. Like I've said, like attracts like. Just make sure our new friends are in alignment with what we want to do in life.

I am giving my perspective on how things played out for me. I'm going to share with you some simple things I did. First, when I say "simple things," making friends isn't simple. It is tough and takes a period of time, but these simple things are a way for us to get our foot in the door. My biggest challenge is, as of this writing, I am fifty-five years old. Most of the people I interact with are twenties to forties. It is just the circles I am engaged with. Most times, I am the oldest in the group. Therefore, connections are more difficult for me, but they do happen.

Our age really doesn't matter. It is who we are and what we bring to the table. Again, Zig Ziglar's quote was "When we go out to be a friend …" Don't seek out friends. Seek out like-minded people and be their friends. Do what you can for them.

Let's find some like-minded friends. Log onto and/or download onto your phone Meetup (www.meetup.com). This is a site/app where you can join a large number of clubs and organizations in your area. There are networking, hiking, business, travel, wine tasting, dragon rowboat, bowling, biking, fishing, and writing clubs, etc.

In January 2019, one of my New Year's resolutions was to meet new people, I went onto Meetup and found a networking group for small businesses. The reason was, at the time, I was completing my MBA; I had learned about large businesses but had little theory and information on small business—one-person operations for instance. This Meetup group was exactly that—small business, one-person operations—and I went to my first meeting in January.

No, it wasn't that simple, not for me at least. I had sent a message to the group organizer trying to see if I would be a good fit. Back to Zig's quote of going out to be a friend, I wasn't focused on that. I was more focused on not wanting to be a disruption to the group based on the fact I was a corporate guy finishing his master's degree with no real practical experience in business.

I remember that first meeting vividly. There were about twenty people sitting around a large table at a bank conference room. The organizer had everyone introduce themselves and say a little about their business. I was scared of public speaking at the time—no friends, no social skills—and was in the middle of the group having to introduce myself. Good news: a majority of the group were beautiful women. Bad news: that intimidated me even more!

It was my turn. "Hi. I'm David. I'm a corporate employee in the insurance industry. I don't have an interest in having my own business; however, I am finishing my MBA and would like to learn from you all." I could barely speak. I was so nervous. I quivered as I spoke. I knew everyone was looking at me like I was a knucklehead and judging me. This was an entrepreneurs group. *Who the heck was I?*

Three years later, I'm still a part of that group. The organizer is also my life coach, Rachel. Many of the people in that group are friends are acquaintances, and along with Rachel, they have been supportive and encouraged me to become who I am today. I don't know if I got lucky finding that particular group, but it turned out to be one of the best things I've ever done. For whatever reason, Rachel befriended me. We had our ups and downs; I didn't talk to her for a while, but it was because I was immature and wasn't at her level of self-awareness. Fortunately, she became a very important part of my life. When you find good people who elevate you, hang on to them.

Recently I asked Rachel why she stayed connected and friends with me. In the beginning, I was a hot mess with no focus or purpose. Her response was she believes everyone comes into our lives for a reason. Some come to be a positive person who contributes to our lives, and others come in to challenge us, to squeeze us and see what were made of. If someone annoys you, what does that say about you? Why do you have the judgment of them as being annoying?

Dr. Wayne Dyer talks about an orange. When you cut open an orange and squeeze it, what comes out? Orange juice. Why doesn't apple juice come out? Because orange juice is inside. When we are squeezed, what comes out? Anger, frustration, judgment? Is that what is inside us? Our response to stimulus will indicate what emotions and feelings we have simmering inside.

I also joined a hiking, camping, and rock climbing group on Meetup, another great group. There are regulars, but it seems every time I go, I meet someone new. In lieu of pumping iron in a gym, I'm out hiking mountains, climbing the sides of cliffs, and camping in the mountains over a mile above sea level. Fresh air, exercise, and good company—what else could you want?

Another option is to join your local Toastmasters club. Toastmasters.org will help you find a club in your local area. This is one of the best things I did for my self-esteem, overcoming my shyness and fear of public speaking and opening up opportunities that I didn't think were possible. If you are thinking, *Oh heck no!* then you are the prime person; you need to do this for you!

Toastmasters is a club whose members are there to overcome their fear of public speaking. I call them superheroes because they are doing the one thing most people on Earth are scared of. Join Toastmasters and be surrounded by superheroes who are motivated, highly energetic, and success oriented. My club is mostly millennials. Again, I'm the old guy in the group. Therefore, we don't hang out, but I love being around them. They bring me up, teach me, and in turn, I do the same for them.

I will tell you it is not a scary as you may think. When you walk in there for the first time, you don't have to give a speech, nor the second, third, or fourth time; it's when you are ready. Toastmasters is organized in such a way to allow you to be a guest and watch, then join, start doing small roles, and when you are ready, start giving speeches.

When I started Toastmasters, I was petrified. I would almost get sick just driving there, parking, and walking in the door. The first time I joined, I was a member for a little over a month; I had a bad speech and then quit out of humiliation. My own humiliation! No one else in the club cared, only me. Round two, I joined again, still scared to death every time I went, but I was committed to making it work. Work and extracurricular activities made it so I had to overcome my fear of public speaking; my promotions and being *voluntold* to do things made public speaking a must!

When you join Toastmasters, and I highly recommend you do, do not quit. My second time around, I started going through the various steps of overcoming my fears. There were three things I vowed never to do: become president of the club, be the "Toastmaster of the Day," and enter speech contests. OK, you know what happened. As of this writing, I am the president of my club, I have been the Toastmaster of the Day more times than I can count, and I have been in two speech contests.

In another chapter, we will discuss dating, but chances are you are currently on dating apps. Do you go out on dates, get disappointed, get in your car, and then delete them before you even leave the parking lot? Yeah, I used to do that too! One of my good friends is a woman I met on a dating app; we went out of a date, didn't have a romantic connection, but did have enough in common to stay in touch. Three-plus years later, we hang out, go to lunch, go hiking, and have good conversations.

Other women whom I've chased but were not interested in me, again, are some of my good friends. They saw value in me. Who knew? I still have a number of women I've gone out with from dating apps or never met in person, yet we are friends on Facebook and Instagram; you never know what happens in the future. My point is it is difficult to meet people you have a connection with; if you've connected on a dating app, you must have something in common to get to a first date. Go into the dating scene with the attitude, at a minimum, you'll make a friend. Communicate that to the other person. It will actually help you and, yes, get you a friend.

This attitude will help us by saying to our perspective date, and by letting her know, if we're not a romantic connection, we can still be friends. This will indicate we don't just want to hook up; we are looking for something real, something in the way of a romantic relationship or a friendship relationship. If a woman is not interested in us romantically, we don't put our tail between our legs and give up. Step up and be a friend.

Support her on her journey to find her ideal mate. And don't do it with hopes she will someday fall for us; that most likely won't happen, but who knows? Be genuine. I chased after this one woman for a while, consistently and persistently; she had no interest in my romantically, but I continued thinking she would. Eventually, I gave up. I was literally exhausted! She wanted to be friends though, and I realized she was the coolest chick in the room; having her as a friend could prove to be beneficial, and it has. I've met great people through her. Again, don't dismiss people because they are not a romantic connection.

In summary, go out to be a friend, not get a friend. Make it about them, not you. Focus on them. Don't try to have everyone focus on you. Studies have shown the more interested you are in someone, asking them questions about them, the nicer and more interesting they think you are! Be genuinely curious about others; see what makes them tick, and find out as much as you can about them. Act as if there will be a test afterward, put your phone in your pocket, and truly focus on them and listen to the stories they tell.

Later, when we recall a story a week or months later, they will be impressed. This is where it gets tricky; this is a two-way street. We want to make friends with someone of substance; therefore, are they taking an interest in us? Are they asking questions about us? Are they looking at their phones while we talk instead of making eye contact? Are they giving us information beyond the generic small talk?

The CEO of the company I work for, which has 1,500 employees, is a master at this; she gives me what I believe is private information. She recalls personal information about my family and me. She seems truly interested, and she makes me feel like her BFF. Obviously, that is not the case, but it is that genuine interest in other people that makes people like you. It is what makes you likeable, a leader, a CEO of a multibillion-dollar company! She might have a three-by-five card with information on every employee that she reads before she talks with them; whatever the case, it works. Personally, I believe she is a truly good person who does care about her employees and the community as a whole.

Cultivating Friendships

This seems simple enough. Once we have some friends, how do we build those friendships into strong bonds? When we were married, our friends were our friends. Basically, as dudes, we had friends we were provided by our wives. The husband of our wife's friend became our friend. We didn't have to work at it; it was what it was. We'd tolerate their quirks and even hang out with people we didn't like that much, just to have time away from our spouse or someone to watch a ball game with. We just needed other male connection and conversation; we needed to be able to hang with the boys and accepted.

Things are different now; we do have choices as do the other guys. They don't have to hang out with us, and we don't have to hang out with them. However, if we encounter someone we enjoy being with and can see them as a friend, here are some suggestions on how to make it a strong connection.

First, a friend has a trait of being loyal. They are always there for us. We can count on them. Be that person for our friends;

answer the phone when they call. If they text with a question or are needing help, pick up the phone and call them; let our friend know it's important to us to respond to them. Be the type of friend we want to have.

Second, be trustworthy; as mentioned earlier, do not repeat gossip or criticize others because our friends will wonder if we do the same to them. We are now achievers; we do not have time to talk about petty things.

Third, be vulnerable with our friends; share what we are feeling, and show our emotions. I will admit most of my friends are women; therefore, it's easier. But the guy friends I have are like-minded, higher level consciously, and achievers. They allow themselves to be vulnerable too. It shows the other we trust him; we are willing to share deep down feelings, emotions, and secrets.

Fourth, give honest feedback. When you join Toastmasters, you'll understand this concept. Feedback at Toastmasters is how we learn and become better public speakers. Yes, it is honest criticism of our speeches, but how else are you going to learn? Same with our friends. We have to give them honest feedback to help them grow but be nice about it. We call it the sandwich approach at Toastmasters; first you give some good points, then some areas for improvement, then follow up with some additional good points.

Fifth, have different friends for different activities. Most of my friends like the same things I do, but we also like to try different things; therefore, it's not that difficult for my main circle of friends to do those different activities. My passion is hiking and camping. Most times, I hike deep into the Appalachian Trail, pitch a tent, and then hike back the next day. This is a strenuous activity. Not all friends want to do that much hiking; therefore, I go solo on most of my trips. When I do shorter hikes/camps, they go with me. The seven-to-ten-mile hikes tend to be solo.

I also like to take cruises; my camping friends don't like structured vacations; they don't want to be confined to a ship. I love cruising, so I go with others. I'm a big Disney fan. My younger daughter currently works there. Again, different friends for Disney. Our friends don't have to do everything we do, nor do they have to include us in everything; be open and not judgmental or jealous when we are not included. Yes, my friends are dumb for not wanting to go on cruises or go to Disney, but I'm not judging!

Sixth, surprise our friends such as by sending a random text; we send cards in the mail, we all practice gratitude; therefore, it's always exciting to get a random gift or note saying how much we are appreciated. No, we're not dating our friends, but we can love and treat them the same as a date, just without the romance. In the beginning, it was odd and creepy; I'd get a random text from a friend saying, "I appreciate you and love you for who you are." I'd take my wallet out and be ready for the next text asking for money, but that next text never came. It was just a genuine communication of gratitude for our friendship.

Why We Need to Be Alone

I love being alone; however, I am an only child. It's in my DNA. I am my own best entertainment; I continually crack myself up! Being alone allows us to power down the system; we don't need to be talking to others, entertaining others, paying attention, or engaging with others. Being alone allows us to reboot our system by just doing nothing. When we are alone, we improve our concentration and become more productive, provided we eliminate the distractions at home.

About five years ago, I got rid of cable. I don't even have a TV in my home anymore. My productivity at work increased so much my boss noticed. I was able to focus on finishing my MBA and taking my life coaching program at the same time. TV drains a lot of our time. If we are going to be alone, be truly alone. At a minimum, turn it off for a few hours and just be alone.

We will become bored if we give up our TV; however, we can pick up a book, take an online course, or just sit and relax listening to music. Getting lost in our thoughts is a great activity; we'll rediscover old goals we had, old ideas, and projects we wanted to do. When we are alone, we can discover things about ourselves such as we're OK being by ourselves. We don't need to rush into another relationship, go out on a date this weekend, or go out with our friends.

Those things are nice, but not having to is an advancement in us. If we are having problems, we can work them out better when we are alone; write them out on a legal pad, sit down, and the answers will come to us. We can't have that clarity if we always have activity and stimulus going on around us.

There are a number of ways experts say we can disconnect, such as waking up a little earlier so we have quiet time, scheduling alone time, closing our office door, turning off our phones, and so on. I spend a majority of my time alone; I don't need to have a schedule or routine to do so. I just do! When I'm in my car, I rarely have the radio on. If I do, it's usually a motivational program. I just drive, focus on my surroundings, and let my mind be clear. Well, until that jerk cuts me off. Then he has my full attention!

There is a difference between being alone and loneliness. Loneliness is when we want to be with others but don't have the social connections to make it happen. Alone is a choice. It is taking time for ourselves; it is solitude for our own well-being. The ability to be alone depends on our personality style as well. If we are lonely, don't choose company that fills the void. Find individuals who will help us positively along the journey of our life. The right friends and social contacts are worth waiting for.[6]

CHAPTER 3

Taking Responsibility

When we know who we are, we will know what to do.
—Unknown

No doubt, this is my favorite chapter because this is where I had my biggest aha moment. I love this chapter because your immediate response to reading "Taking Responsibility" is most likely "Oh heck no! It was her fault. She created all of the problems. She cheated on me. She ..." Yes, yes, she did, but maybe you had a little something to do with it?

Now I'm not belittling your situation; I am having a little fun with you because for four years, it was my belief my ex-wife was 100 percent the reason we got divorced. It was after working with my life coach, being honest with myself, and asking the why questions that I realized I was mostly responsible for our marriage ending.

I'm not going to try to analyze your marriage; that's hard to do writing a book and not knowing your story. I'm not going to try to convince you you're to blame for the issues in your marriage. What I am going to do is tell you my story, including how I went from blaming my ex-wife 100 percent to taking most of the responsibility on myself. My story won't be the same as yours, maybe not even remotely close; however, what I'd like you to do is see how things played out in my self-assessment and see if there is something similar in your situation.

What I would like you to do is think of other options, other possibilities than you currently have. After my story, we'll talk about why it's important to self-assess and come to some kind of answer. We're guys. We need to figure stuff out; why a marriage ends might be overly confusing or what we perceive as a cut-and-dry issue. Keep an open mind because you don't want to repeat the same patterns, if you want to have a successful relationship in the future, you've got to figure this part out. And if you come to the realization you might have contributed to the ending of your relationship, it will be a relief. You'll have some clarity.

My story of taking responsibility was a long process, but I eventually had that aha moment when I figured it out. After my divorce, if you asked me what happened, I would have told you that my wife is a Cuban with a hot Latin temper. We fought all the time, literally all the time, and after eighteen years, I got tired of it. It was that final argument took me over the edge.

That was my story, that was my reality, and that was what I believed. She was bad. I was good. Deep down, I knew I was part to blame; it takes two to fight and argue. She'd say something, I'd say something, and off to the races we'd go. Over the years, the fights got nastier and more personal. It was that final argument where I got up close, looked her in the eyes, and wanted to knock her block off; I knew that was the end, this couldn't continue. I asked for the divorce, the hardest thing I've ever done.

Over time, I still blamed her. Eventually, for whatever reason, I took responsibility for the marriage. I told her I was responsible for the failure and I wore that badge on my shirt for about a year. I took full responsibility, not really knowing why but accepting the fact I must have done something wrong.

Then, in a session with my life coach, she asked what type of woman I was looking for. She knew I was not successful at dating and dating was not a priority. Therefore, she asked me to write down my ideal woman, a head-to-toe, heart-to-brain description of the type of woman I wanted in my life. I attempted to do this; however, I kept getting stuck with the obvious, my ex-wife. We were together twenty-five years, married eighteen, she was my reference point. She had the look and attributes I wanted and liked, because she's what I had for half of my life. I concluded I want my ex-wife, just nicer.

It's amazing when you start focusing on things how the universe will give you the answers or bring the right people into your life. A few days after I was doing this exercise and struggling to define what type of woman I wanted in my life, I met a nice Ukrainian lady on a dating app, and we decided to meet right away. It was during COVID-19 when everything was closed; we were to go for a walk on a greenway to get to know each other. As it turned out, the closed restaurant we were to meet at had actually opened that very day for the first time. We decided to sit down for dinner and drinks, outside on the roof, overlooking the river; it was a perfect and beautiful night.

I was immediately attracted to my new Ukrainian friend; she was a cute, petite brunette, my age, with a killer body as she was into ballroom dancing. She also had a cute accent, but not too heavy. Additionally, she had a master's degree in education. On the outside, she was checking all of the boxes.

As we spoke, there were some differences in our personalities such as our love languages. My number one is physical touch, then quality of time, and finally positive affirmations. Those were not hers, and the differences set me back a little, but I was still interested. She then told me what she was looking for, and this is where it gets good.

She wants to get married again. She had gotten divorced ten years ago in Ukraine and moved to America with her daughter. Being a European, she wanted the traditional relationship where the man is the man and the woman supports him. Not that she does what he says, but her role is the wife, and the man takes care of everything. He is, by definition, the man of the house.

While married, my wife wore the pants in the house; she took care of everything. I had lost my manliness; I became a typical TV character who kept his head down and did what I was told. Overall, life was good, we had a good lifestyle, nice vacations, homes, cars, private school for the girls, but my ex handled everything.

My new Ukrainian friend is what I wanted in a woman. I wanted to be the man! I wanted to take care of my woman. I wanted to hold her hand, not have her take my hand and guide me. I wanted to be the type of guy who could be the man. That was my epiphany; it was right there in front of me. I literally laughed out loud because this is what my life coach and I were looking for. What did I want in my life as it relates to a relationship? She just gave me the answer.

Now that I had the blueprint of the type of woman I wanted, I thought, *Yes, a European woman; they are more traditional than American women, where they want the man to be the man.* Then I thought, *Well, Latin women are also like that,* so I narrowed it down to a European or a Latin woman.

Don't get ahead of me, because if you paid attention above, you know my ex-wife is a Cuban, a Latin woman. This is where the aha moment came into play. This is where I realized why the marriage failed; this is where I realized my responsibility, pretty much 100 percent for things not working out. And it is these kinds of revelations that I hope will provide you with clarity to make you understand your role in what happened and, like me, express it to your ex to give her the peace of mind that you finally get it.

We finally hear everything she had been saying, yelling, and screaming at us for years. We finally understand all of the things the therapists had said to us that we didn't hear or comprehend. For me, the answers and solutions were out there, I just didn't see or hear them.

When I realized I wanted a Latin woman with a traditional marriage mindset, I realized I had had one. That was who my wife was; that is the type of marriage she wanted. However, due to my failing early on in the marriage, she had to step up and take charge; she had to do the finances, pay the bills, make the tough decisions, do the planning, buy the house and cars, etc. She became the man of the house. And the more she had to do, the more I stopped doing; she was forced into a role she didn't want to have.

It was a role reversal that was created by my inactions. For eighteen years, my wife had to do everything. Yes, I worked and contributed to the family; I believe I was a great dad, I loved my wife, always held her hand, kissed her, and adored her. At some point though, I just lost the feeling of being the man, of having my own destiny. On the flip side, my wife wanted to be a woman, she wanted a man to take care of everything, unfortunately she didn't have that relationship. She was resentful, bitter, angry, and regularly lashed out. I thought she was just a mean person, always angry, and that hot Latin temper didn't help!

My realization was I truly was responsible for the marriage turning out the way it did due to my failures early on as a man. It was a relief, it was peace of mind, and it was something I expressed to my ex along with an apology. Yes, I had taken responsibility for the failure of the marriage a long time ago; however, I now knew why.

It was an eye-opener to my whole adult life, it was sad, yet it was also inspiring. I knew what my failures were; now I could move forward knowing not only what I want but how to make sure I and my future partner have it. Even with my Ukrainian friend, I knew I was not the man she needed; it made me think how I could become that person. That in and of itself was also a growth in my life. I hadn't been a man in twenty years, and now is my time.

Although the Ukrainian and I didn't work out, we still remain friendly acquaintances. As mentioned, it was a learning experience; she was the woman I wanted, but I wasn't the man she needed. Not at that point in time, maybe not even now, but I am working toward being that man. It is when we can look in the mirror and honestly acknowledge our strengths and weaknesses that we have growth. It's when we realize where we are lacking and are willing to make the changes needed that we become the man worthy of a quality woman.

Here are some reasons why you need to take responsibility.

Take responsibility; truly understand what failures we had in the marriage. Embrace them, share them with our exes, and determine how we can fix and improve upon them. Then we can live a happy life with someone wonderful; that should be our aim.

What value does take responsibility have in our life? Once we honestly evaluate our life, our marriage, and take responsibility, we become in charge of our life. Even if we come to the discovery I did—that I played a very big role in the ending of the marriage based on my actions—we will have such a relief! It has been a huge weight off my shoulders.

We then go from being the victim of our marital circumstances to the victor in our life. Instead of reacting to everything that comes our way, we are in control; we have a new swagger about ourselves.

When we figure out what happened in our relationship, we stop blaming our exes. As long as we blame our exes, rightfully so or not, we are victims. If we continue to blame her for everything, we are the victim; we allowed this to happen to us. Realizing and taking responsibility means we made mistakes, acknowledge them, and are now in charge.

It becomes difficult for us to move forward if we always have an excuse; blaming our exes for our woes is an excuse. Then we get into an excuse mode; every time something comes up, we find an excuse to get out of it, not to take responsibility or deal with it head-on. When we stop blaming, we can decide what to do when an issue does come up. There is no one else to use as a crutch; it's on us.

Similar to blaming, complaining is another negative we need to conquer. When we complain, especially about things our exes did or do, we give them control. We are saying we have no control or choice, and therefore we just complain about it. Come on, man. Stop blaming others for events in our life; start taking control, take responsibility, and when the poop hits the fan, deal with it. Stop giving our exes so much relevance and power by complaining about them. Catch what they're throwing out, deal with it, and let it go; don't give them any of our time or energy.

We have heard it and we know we need to practice it: live in the moment. Put down our cell phones and focus on who we are currently with or what we are currently doing. We can't give our kids quality time if we are looking at our phones while talking to them. The problem is if we are living in the past and festering about our marriage, we cannot live in the present.

Now we know when we've figured it out, once we get to that realization, we will become more confident people. We're guys, we like to figure things out, know how they work, and do not ask for help. Therefore, we need to do this self-assessment and truly find out our role. When we do, our life will change; it will be a hard pill to swallow, but we become more of a man. We will get rid of that uncertainty because we'll know the facts.

There will be no more doubt or uncertainty in the back of our mind as to what happened. I'm not saying we'll discover we were to blame, but if we do an honest assessment, we'll know, and when we know, we'll have some peace of mind.

With peace of mind, confidence, and a strong foundation, we will open our mind to discover our life purpose. We might think we know our life purpose, but we probably don't; we have been focused too much on the past, on blaming and complaining. If we have set some goals or found our purpose, chances are they are safe. They aren't the ones we truly want and deserve. Closing out that chapter of our life but closing it where we feel good and confident about the outcome will allow us to move forward, not on. Moving forward will make us realize we do not need to accept whatever is given to us; we decide where we are going along our journey of life.

CHAPTER 4

Self-Love, Loving Yourself

You can't give to others what you don't acknowledge you have.
—Elinor Miller

What my friend Elinor means is we can't love someone else unless we love ourselves first. Or at least acknowledge that we love ourselves. It's probably been a while since we have looked in the mirror to love and appreciate the person we see. If we do not have love, how can we give it?

That is why I am putting this chapter before the chapter on dating. Like attracts like; if we are a hot mess emotionally from our divorce or separation, we will attract a hot mess into our life. We don't want a hot mess; we want someone awesome. We need to be awesome to attract awesome and therefore need to start working on ourselves.

Think of it like remodeling a house. How much work needs to be done? Do we need to go all the way down to the foundation and start over? Or can we add a new coat of paint and some new ceiling fans? What is the degree of rehab that needs to be done?

The same applies with us; maybe we came out of the divorce in pretty good shape—emotionally at least. But to put that house on the market, we need some curb appeal. All of this information won't all apply to everyone, but it might give us that little edge. For those of us who need to go to the foundation, this is a good start but not the end of our journey. A book is a good guidepost but definitely cannot provide us all the skills we need. This book should provide us with direction as to where to go in order to continue our growth. Either way, read on, my friends.

Self-love: we have to learn to love ourselves before we can love others; we should accept and love ourselves before we start dating.

What is self-love, and why do we need to do it?

Self-love is not vanity, conceded, or egotistical; self-love is when we truly love ourselves. It is when we look in the mirror and like the person we see truly, deeply, and unconditionally. Most of us love our children unconditionally; that is the level of love we refer to. We need to look in the mirror and have that same amount of love for ourselves.

For many of us, we've fallen out of love for ourselves. Marriage, kids, life, work, mortgage, obstacles, failures in life, divorce—we have a different perception of ourselves than we should have. It's all understandable; many divorced men feel like they have been beaten up for years. They have lost their masculinity or manliness, have filed their goals and dreams away, and have lost their roar! We will work on all of these things throughout this book; however, step one is to love ourselves.

What exactly does that mean? When I started working with my life coach, there were times I loved myself and there were times I didn't. For instance, when I was on dating apps and had a stable full of women I was talking to and was able to go out of different dates on a regular basis, I loved myself. When my "likes" were empty, I had self-doubt and didn't like myself. When things were going well at work, when I was out having fun with friends, losing weight, getting new clothes, getting a new hairstyle, when all of the traffic got out of my way, I loved myself. When things were not working out, I again got into a funk and didn't like the person in the mirror.

The outside influences made me feel good and worthy. Self-love is an internal feeling and belief; all of the outside influences make us feel warm and fuzzy or sad and blue. If we have self-love, we are always OK and happy with who we are. Most importantly, those outside influences can go away, and where is our self-esteem then? During the COVID-19 situation, did we all gain weight? Did we date much? How was our single life self-esteem?

If we have had trouble dating or finding an ideal person to have in our lives, we are more than likely dealing with low self-love. The saying is "We can't love someone else until we love ourselves first." That is an important phrase to remember and to continually work on.

On the dating apps, we may find that like attracts like. The women who "like" us are more than likely similar to us, such as the same age range, same weight, and same interest. It also transmits our self-love; if we don't love ourselves, we will attract someone who doesn't love themselves, and we will be in a hot mess of a relationship. Yay! Fun! Another hot mess to date!

We may find someone, or we might be the someone who says, "I'm miserable, I'm unhappy, but you make me happy. You bring me up!" Doesn't that sound wonderful? What would that relationship look like? Needy, clingy, negative—everything we do not want.

What does it mean to have self-love? When we love ourselves, we know what we want in life; we have clarity as to the direction of our life. Our goals, the rules that guide us, and the desires we have. Once we have this foundation, we can focus on the important things—our goals—and not be distracted by impulse items or choices that take us in a different direction.

When we love ourselves, we take better care of ourselves; we eat better and make different choices. In one of his songs, Jimmy Buffet says, "I treat my body like a temple, you treat yours like a tent." Are we treating our body (eating and exercising) like the temple it is, or are we just throwing junk in there and not giving it much thought?

When we love and care for ourselves; we exercise and have a different work ethic. We may have different views on dating and overall have a different attitude. But the other good thing is we can eat a box of Milk Duds and be OK with our choice. When we have clarity, through self-love, we know what is best for us; we are able to say no to work and social activities that don't move us toward our goals.

When we're in a good place, our circle of friends changes. We attract and manifest the people into our life that will provide value and move us in the right direction. I have spoken about our circle of friends in a previous chapter. There is a saying "When the student is ready, the teacher will arrive." This can be friends or a romantic interest who comes into our life and changes the trajectory for the better. In order for this to happen though, we need to be in a good place with ourselves.

One of the more difficult things, at least for me, is to forgive ourselves for previous actions and failures. When we have as many as I do, it can be difficult. What we need to do is look at the mistakes made in our life as a learning opportunity. Everything happens in life for a reason, and we are where we are right now because of those actions, those mistakes, and those accomplishments. I'd like to address the statement "Everything happens in life for a reason." It happens because of our actions, planning, or lack of planning. Things don't just happen; there is a cause and an effect.

And I know this sounds like a contradiction to my first chapter where I said everything does not happen for a reason. That first chapter was a reference to our emotional well-being—the difficulties we are going through in our divorce, separation, or loss. In the overall theme of the universe and being a spiritual person, I believe things do happen for a reason. But individual and specific things are not a broad stroke in the journey of our lives.

This past weekend, I met Wilson, and sometimes you meet people who are not thought leaders. They are just regular dudes doing what they do. Wilson is in construction and the conversation of dating and self-love came up. Wilson said and showed in a most dramatic way. Wilson is Latin. They talk with their whole bodies, not just hands. Latins will stand up to tell a story and move around using gestures. Anyway, Wilson said he had to learn to love himself and to learn to accept the good and the bad parts. He then bent over, scooped up the bad on one side and the good on the other, hugged them, and brought them into his chest. He embraced the good and the bad of his life. It's who he is, it's what he is, and it's where he is in his life.

My life coach gave me an exercise to start loving myself. This is not a one-and-done exercise, it takes work and commitment;

we have to do it daily for months until we truly learn to love ourselves. We stand in front of a mirror, look at ourselves, and say, "I love you." At first, we're going to say, "Yeah right," or "No, I don't!" Or something snarky like that. That's OK, eventually we'll get past that. It takes time. For me, I would look in the mirror, see a few extra pounds around my waist and in my face, and it was difficult to love myself. (Those are superficial things and have nothing to do with who we are.)

My life coach then told me to get closer to the mirror, where I'd only see my face, or closer, where I only saw my eyes and nose, and then I could just see me. I didn't have to worry about the extra pounds. It was just me looking at myself, and then I started the daily process of saying, "I love you." Every day, looking in the mirror, up close. After a while, I'd walk by and look at myself in a full-length mirror, and I was OK because after a while, we learn to love ourselves.

It took me a while, but I'm OK looking at myself in the mirror and saying it. This process is something we need to do daily. In the beginning, have fun with it. Over time, we'll look deep into our eyes and feel it. We will get it; it will come to us. And when we finally love ourselves, things will start to change; we will see and feel the difference in ourselves. Then life starts to change for the good.

Another step is to do the things to become the man we want to be. Or more desirable, be the man far beyond who we thought we could be. Once we are that person, we can't help but love ourselves. Taking the advice, learning, and taking action to make changes will inevitably change who we are; as we change, we are going to think we are kind of a cool guy. Then when we are at that point, it gets good because we start trying and doing things way out of our scope of possibility. Once you start to do these knew things, you keep going and trying even newer things. It is the snowball effect.

We all want more in our lives, more success, more things to impress others. But why do we want them? Chances are because on the inside we believe we are less. We are trying to find self-love through impressing ourselves with more success, accomplishments, and material things. Yes, we do these things to impress others; however, we're also doing them to impress ourselves. Get to the point where we don't need to impress ourselves because we know we are awesome; then we will stop trying to impress others.

We need to create a standard for ourselves to be happy all the time. We need to believe we can. Make a strategy to be happy all the time. How can we do that? How can we decide to be happy all of the time? Just decide to. Other emotions such as depression we have to work to put ourselves into. We do not get depressed; we do depression. It is the way we hold our bodies, the way we breathe, the thoughts we have, the things we say. These are all the things we are doing, and then once we have them done, we are depressed. Yay! That was a lot of work, but we got there!

See yourself as extraordinary, and you will create an extraordinary life. See yourself as defeated and sad, and you'll also create that life. I'm not saying it's easy, but if you have a choice, which you do, choose to be happy. It's easier to work through your problems when you are happy and able to think a little differently than when you are sad or mad. Again, we do not feel an emotion; we do an emotion.

I am sure we have all heard the song "YMCA" by the Village People. Well, now we will be humming that song for the next few hours; it's contagious. It is called an incantation whereby we hear something over and over and it sticks in our mind—even

"YMCA," which is from 1978. Usually, it's a song or a line from a movie or TV show we saw long ago; it is a little something that sticks in our mind. The negative incantations are those self-talk items, such as "I can't, and therefore you won't." When we repeat over and over that we cannot do something, our mind believes us, and if we try it and fail, our mind says, "See, I told you so." Self-love is saying and knowing we can and then doing it. It's not automatic. We have to work at everything in life, but just believe we can, and we will.

It takes the same energy to be negative or positive; it is the same physiology. As mentioned, I'm a Toastmaster; the same feeling I have when I get up to give a speech and I'm nervous are the same feelings I have when I'm excited to get up and give a speech. For me, when I'm nervous, I tell myself that I must be excited and energized to give the speech. The same emotions are pumping through my body that are giving me butterflies, getting my heart racing, and making me more focused on who's in the room. That can be a negative or a positive; I choose to make it a positive.

There is only one thing that determines how we feel, and that is the way we communicate to ourselves. The way we change our communication with ourselves is to ask a better question. Master the communication we have with ourselves. Most of us allow others to tell us what to thing or do. They let us know how to feel. If we do not control our thoughts, someone else will. Nothing in life has meaning except the meaning we give it.

Loving ourselves is a difficult exercise, a difficult task. Unfortunately, once we love ourselves, something or someone is going to come along and make us question it. We will be passed up for promotions; we will be dumped by someone we really like; something will happen with the kids or our parents where they set us back. We find ourselves saying, "Why me?" It is these challenging times where we have growth in loving ourselves. We can show ourselves what we are made of.

If a friend was down in the dumps and said, "Why me?" what would we say? We might say, "It's not you. You're fine. It's just a few unfortunate events that you need to handle." Talk to ourselves like we talk to our friends. We deserve to have someone believe in us and encourage us. That person should be ourselves.

In the 2014 movie *The Equalizer,* Denzel Washington (Robert McCall) is talking to Chloe Grace Moretz (Teri). She says something like "That's just how the world is." Denzel then says, "Change your world." What is changing our world? It's changing our mindset; it's changing our beliefs. Love ourselves, know we are worthy, and we can accomplish and handle anything.

CHAPTER 5

Dating

No matter how attractive a person's potential
may be, you have to date their reality.
—Mandy Hale

The only fact I know without a doubt when it comes to
dating is I have no idea how to make it work. Many times, I
thought I found the surefire way to navigate the dating scene
only to be disappointed on a date, get dumped, or get snookered
by someone. If someone says they have the magic beans to help
us in our dating ventures, hide our wallet. We are about to be
conned. This dating app is not better than that dating app. This
approach is not better than that approach; it all comes down to
that face-to-face meeting with a stranger we are interested in. So
many variables need to come into play for us to connect.

Once we connect, it is a long journey of discovering each
other's quirks, triggers, likes, and dislikes. Then there are the
rules—their rules and our rules. We all have rules that we
commonly refer to as "red flags." When someone breaks our
rules for how we operate our life, or when we break their rules,

they throw up the red flags. The longer we are single and have settled into our routine, the more rules we will have. In turn, it will be hard to let someone into our life. Even more difficult will be for us to allow ourselves into someone else's life. We are going to have to change and break some of our own rules.

I like my life of solitude exactly the way it is. To go out on a date, I have to change my routine. I have to iron a shirt, go out and spend two to four hours of my valuable time, and spend a hundred or so dollars that could pay down a credit card or be invested in lieu of being flushed down the toilet. I then have to text and call, again taking my focus away from my routine, my rules. Actually, I'm probably not the best person to talk about dating, but I'm here so I'll do it!

Almost all dates are the same conversation: telling a complete stranger our life story to see if they like us, to see if they approve of the choices we have made. How many times after a date or two do we completely regret telling someone our life story? Now that person we no longer talk to is out there with the knowledge of our life. They might know our kid's name, our personal secrets, where we work, and our manager's name. We give out so much information to try to attract a mate. But what's the solution? There isn't one, that's just how the process works.

There is a comedian named Sam Morril who did a routine about dating that I loved. He said when we meet someone, we ask what type of music they like, if we don't like that music we need to decide if we can coexist with them. His new first-date question is one I think I'll start using. "How likely are you to yell at me in public?" That is good information to know in advance.

Now let's talk about that dreaded subject. We are going to talk about dating apps, or dating in general, but it seems dating entails dating apps.

Meeting people is more difficult now, especially during the COVID-19 situation, but in general, it seems unlikely that we can walk up to someone in a bar and pick them up. That seems so archaic, and with the me-too movement and respecting a woman's space, how dare we walk up and say hello? Therefore, dating apps seem the way to go.

Over the past four to five years, I've dated a lot, learned a lot, and gotten frustrated and confused *a lot!* I've been trying to figure out the secret to successful dating on dating apps.

As you all know, women tend to post pictures of themselves when they used to be really good-looking. Or say they like certain activities and hobbies when in fact they have only done them once. For instance, a common picture of an "adventurous" woman is skydiving, when they are in tandem with the instructor. The picture I'd like to see is them skydiving without the instructor; they have taken the classes and jumped a number of times, whatever the qualifications. But that one-time thing does not define them. Nor does it define us.

I believe I do have the secret to successfully dating and more specifically finding that ideal mate who we can see ourselves with over the long haul. I'm just kidding. I wrote this when I thought I had the silver bullet to dating, then I was dumped; therefore, I don't have all the answers. But let's go through the exercise anyway. Maybe I just had bad luck and all of you will be more fortunate.

If we are just looking to date and don't want anything serious, then we know what to do: keep swiping right and keep going out and having fun. There is nothing wrong with that, as long as we realize it's our intent. That is not where I'm at. I'm looking for that someone special, and as of this writing, I believe I've found her. (Not! Dumped shortly after writing that.) (Update. As of today, I have found that someone special who I believe is in it for the long haul. At a minimum, at least until the book is published.)

First, make an avatar of our perfect woman, including what she looks like, what her height is, what her nationality or region she's from is, what her age range is, what her education or career status is, what her religious or political views are, what her temperament is, and so on. We need the perfect avatar of a woman we would like to be with. Do we have that image—those qualities she possesses, that person we want to be with?

Second, are we ready to meet her? Are we in a good space where we can welcome a woman into our life and heart and begin to start a relationship? If not, go back to swiping right and being a serial dater. If we don't want to be a serial dater but are not in a space to welcome a woman into our heart, continue reading this book and we'll get there. I dated a number of awesome women over the years, but I wasn't in a good space; I got scared of the routine, which reminded me of my marriage, and I ended it. I've had to kick myself for letting those women go, but it was in their best interest to get away from me.

Third, stop swiping right on women who don't match that avatar. Even if a hot lady likes us first and we go, "Wow, I want to date her," if she is not in the realm of our avatar, it's a waste of our time and her time, not to mention a waste of your money. Have we all figured out dating is expensive?

It may take some time, but she will show up. We have to be patient. And be a little creative. For instance, my ideal woman is between the ages of forty-five and fifty-two. For some reason, I decided to set my parameters for forty to fifty-five just to see who shows up. My lady showed up as forty-two years old, but she's actually forty-four; she messed up her settings when she did the original profile and can't change it back, and she turns forty-five in a few months. She is literally an image of my avatar, and she even came with an added perk: I like camping and hiking, as does she. But she used to be in the army reserves and really knows how to hike and camp! (Yes! She dumped me too. She wasn't that good at hiking or camping anyway!)

Dating apps. Can we believe we are talking about and having to deal with dating apps? Dating apps seem to be the way to meet someone. I've met a few great people on them, I've had a few duds, and I've made a few friends. My biggest advice is if we find someone we connect with "on paper" but don't connect with in person, don't write them off. Keep them as friends. Life is better with friends.

I have half a dozen people I've met on dating apps who I'm still either friends with or connect with on Facebook and talk to occasionally. Actually, I have a couple of close friends who I was initially attracted to; it didn't work out romantically, meaning there wasn't even a first kiss, but we're still friends today. Don't write them off, plus have the mindset they have friends who we might connect with. Network in business, life, and romance. Obviously, if there is zero connection, this might not apply.

Research on the Rules of Dating from Actual Women

These rules come from women I've met who tell me horror stories about guys they have met on dating apps. They have told me their likes and dislikes for profiles and dating. Overall, guys behave really poorly. I hope those reading are not one of them. I mean I'm really shocked at how badly men behave on a first date. *What's wrong with them?* That's good news for guys like me; if I brush my teeth, comb my hair, and act halfway decent, I'm way ahead of the curve.

The first thing, and it's hard—really, really hard (that's what she said)—is not to talk about our exes. Understandably, she was our best friend and partner for a large percentage of our life. She is our reference point to just about everything. Any conversation we have, any story we want to tell or share, will most likely include her. We have to pace ourselves. Don't have diarrhea of the mouth; become a mystery man, pause, and think about our answers. If our answers include our exes, think of an alternative way to tell the story.

My last girlfriend (OK, my last, last, last girlfriend as of this writing), one of the reasons we stopped dating was that I talked about my ex too much; she was convinced I wanted to get back with her. The lady I was dating was a younger, sexier, awesome lady, and the thought of leaving her and going back with my ex blew my mind. That was her feeling though based on countless conversations that I should not have had—stories I should not have told, true feelings about my ex that I should not have shared. And talking bad about our exes isn't any better. It shows us as being petty, resentful, having regret, and not having the ability to move on. Do not talk about exes!

Second, do not talk about politics or religion. This goes not only for dating but life and business in general. It's one of those golden rules: don't talk about politics or religion in polite company.

Personally, I've had so many awakenings when it comes to issues such as this. I have an acquaintance who is very liberal, like she will cut your head off if you talk positively about Trump, yet she's currently in a relationship with a guy who supports Trump. Go figure! They are a good connection with common interests, and in the end, the politics are a bickering point but not a deal breaker for them. So again, don't write everyone off we don't agree with, and even easier, don't talk politics or religion at the beginning of meeting people.

I can remember a lady I was talking with. We seemed like a good connection, and then I brought up the question of her political affiliation. We were the same; however, it just got weird after that because it was an issue that didn't need to be brought up. It was irrelevant to every conversation we had, it wasn't a concern on either side, but for whatever reason, I went there, and it backfired.

Some women do post their strong religious or political view on the dating apps; if they are opposite of ours, we might not be a connection. I have found that after talking for a while and maybe even a date or two, we discover there are differences, but be the bigger man and put it aside. Tell her it's a conversation for another day and we will cross that bridge when we get there. I've dated some women whose dating profiles indicate they love themselves some Jesus, but after a few dates, that's actually not a priority. Again, proceed with caution and try to avoid the subject.

Third, don't talk about ourselves too much! I actually had a lady tell me, "Wow, you share a lot, don't you?" Go back to that chapter about self-love. "Yeah, I'm awesome and I'm going to tell everyone I meet." Maybe not the best idea. When we are talking about ourselves, we are not gaining information about her. Let her do the talking. Ask her open-ended questions. The first few dates are data-gathering exercises. Be a sleuth, be interested in her by asking questions, and direct the conversation to items we want to find out about. Plus when we ask people about them and they get to talk about themselves, they tend to think *we* are interesting.

Fourth, my friends complain about our pictures not being true representations of ourselves. Really? I've yet to meet a woman with current or accurate pictures that have not been taken with filters. I can go off in a dozen directions about women and their profile pictures, but let's keep our focus and just say try to let them know who we are.

If we are on dating apps now, go look at our pictures; are they more than three to six months old? If so, delete them. Take off our ratty, old T-shirt, put on a polo or dress shirt, and do some selfies, close-ups, and full-body shots. Speaking of photos, believe it or not, I've never met a woman who likes a picture of us fishing and showing off our catch; when we are hunting or our kill, our truck, nor our sports car. Our pictures should present us, nothing but us.

The experts say we should wait at least a year before we start dating. It's difficult to wait, but I would agree. As mentioned earlier, I met a number of wonderful women early on after my separation, but I got scared and ended the relationships. Yes, if I would have waited a year, I wouldn't have met them, but the outcome is the same today; I am alone and not with them. The only difference is I have a few women out there who are pissed at me for breaking up with them! My advice would be to wait, feel comfortable being alone, and rediscover ourselves. That is what this book is all about.

Is it OK not to date and be alone? Back to our experts, who say we need human contact, human relationships, and companionship. Those who are in relationships or married tend to live longer than single people. I'm fine being alone, being single, but then again, I'm an only child so solitude is in my DNA. I would agree. It is better to have someone in our life, but if we are coming out of a divorce or breakup, make sure the next one is the one. We are worth the wait. We don't have to rush into a relationship with every girl we meet—says the guy who after a couple of weeks dating someone posted on Facebook he was in a relationship! What a dork! Don't do that, because, as expected, it ended a few weeks later. Geez, I've made some bad choices along the way, but they were learning experiences. Learn from me! Don't do these things.

I'm at the point in my life where I have a lot of women friends. Yes, I am in the dreaded friend zone. The good thing is I have incredible women around me all the time. No, there is no romance or sex; there are just some fun and interesting people to hang out with. If I started dating, it would make things awkward; how would this new person fit into my tribe of friends? Would I lose my friends because they don't like this new person? This all goes back to the chapter on friends.

But it also goes to what I said above in this chapter about staying friends with women, even if you are not a romantic connection. One of my friends is setting me up on a date in a couple of weeks; we are going to meet for dinner and drinks, the three of us. We'll see how that changes this chapter; as I've dated, I have had to go in and edit out scenarios, advice, and people from the book because things didn't work out. One of the great things about being friends and just hanging out as friends is we don't have to worry about Valentines or anniversary gifts. We go Dutch when we go out for dinner, drinks, or other events. Yeah, I can be cheap.

Well, a follow-up to the above paragraph. Yes, my friend set me up on a date with an awesome lady, someone who I was automatically attracted to. OK, you know it didn't work out. I was really upset with her because I spent over $1,000 in dinners over a three-week period. She knew she didn't like me after the first or second date, but she allowed me to keep taking her out to nice places. And I kept taking this lady out to dinner even though we didn't kiss. I think we both felt an obligation to our mutual friend to give it a try. Do you know how much Bitcoin I could have bought with $1,000? Yeah, $1,000 worth!

Why do we date anyway? To find a companion, someone to marry? Dating is a path to a relationship, it's a path that we need to experience and be patient with. How many times have we met a woman, thought she was awesome and we were a perfect match and just want to lock this one down so no one else gets her? I think my count is about a dozen. Then it doesn't work out. My problem is I rush. I meet an awesome woman and just want to be with her. For whatever reason, that hasn't worked out for me, nor does it seem to be the path.

My training and education tell me to take it slowly because over time, we will discover different things about them, and they will discover things about us. For instance, if we start dating in January and things are wonderful and awesome, how will we feel in February when she has big expectations of us as her new man and we disappoint? Or we go all out for Valentine's Day and she doesn't seem to appreciate the effort. What are November and December going to be like with her around the holidays? Is she included at the Thanksgiving table with our daughters and parents? What about Christmas? Is she ready to meet our exes and our grandkids? Talking about these things months in advance is not a good idea either; it tends to freak them out. Yes, I know because I've found out the hard way!

The worst word is *settle*. We settle because she seems good enough, we are tired of the dating scene, and we are compatible. Settle, compatible, good enough, ugh, that sounds horrible! We are looking to be an awesome person now that we are single, and we do not settle. Relationships are hard, dating is hard, it's what we do, it's what we have to do, it's part of the journey of life. Meet women, take our time to get to know them, don't commit to a relationship right away, but keep things going. If she is rushing us for a relationship, something is up. I'll tell a couple of stories; yeah, I've got lots of stories, as do all of us! Wait until I get my podcast going. We'll have some fun then!

Jane Doe was probably the best-looking, sexiest, and most sexual woman I ever dated. There are too many complexities to put into this book, but we eventually went out on a date after meeting on a dating app. Sitting in a mostly empty restaurant, I was infatuated with this woman based on her looks. Yet I was literally looking at the ceiling, it had metal joist and a metal decking, wishing it would cave in. She was so vapid that I couldn't take the conversation anymore. I asked for the check after the second drink and she got a little pissed.

Her response was to grab my hand and put it down her blouse; she then began to make out with me. That was kind of hot, and the evening got more interesting. Being the dumb guy I am, we went out on a second date, which did not go much better. It was a few weeks from Thanksgiving; I was going to my older daughter's house and my date suggested I take her with me. She wanted to go meet my daughter and grandkids after our second date. That was a hard no! Even if I thought that would be a good idea (because I'm a guy), my daughter would never let a lady I knew for a few weeks in her house with her kids.

It was nonnegotiable, it wasn't going to happen. Well, as we stood outside in the rain having this discussion, she went to her bag of tricks and it was game on again. I never saw her again; she was much more of a hot mess than I was. She also had one kid in college and two high school seniors about to attend college. She was broke. I'm not saying she was looking for someone to help her out financially, but she was.

I am reluctant to talk about Jane Doe number two because we run in the same circles, but let's just say, and this is my perception of the situation, it was a financial decision on her part. The relationship was rushed because she was having some financial hardships and needed a guy (any guy) with a good job, and I guess, that I was good enough. That one didn't work out. And as of this writing, yet another woman I dated seemed wonderful and loving. Yet she was in the process of being evicted, unknown to me. I'm not saying that's why she was dating me, but she and her child had to find a new place to live.

Point is when we meet someone and they want to rush the relationship, there is probably something going on with them. It's not the norm for a woman to want to rush things. They are smarter than we are; they take their time and are cautious along the journey of dating. Looking at it from that perspective, when we (guys) rush a relationship, what does that look like to them? Are we desperate, do we just want sex, are we broke and need a good woman with a job? All of those questions are going through their minds because we are rushing.

Yes, it is difficult to take things slowly when we meet someone awesome, someone we have great chemistry with, someone that we think is our happily ever after; however, we have to. We have to take it slowly. I've had a number of happily ever after woman who did not end up happily ever after because I rushed it.

Finally, dating apps are not the only way to meet someone. Dating apps are what we are used to, something where we can get an immediate response from; we can literally have a date the same or next day. That where our society is. We want it now! We want feedback, results, and we want them now. Dating apps give us that, but if we are single and have been on a dozen dates, let's look at some other options because those women from the dating apps obviously have not worked out.

Recently, I had the mindset of being a bachelor for the rest of my life. I was content with my routine and not having to do the dating thing. I was not on dating apps when a friend wanted to introduce me to one of her friends. It was a true blind date. She was wonderful, beautiful, and checked all of the boxes. No, it did not work out; we were not in alignment. But an interesting thing happened after that. I was still not on dating apps, yet the next four women I dated came into my life randomly. And each woman literally came into my life within a day or two after the last ended. It was an odd situation.

Once it ended with the woman who liked me taking her out to dinner, I got a random Facebook message from a woman I had never met before. We started talking and ended up dating for a few months. A few days after that relationship ended, a woman I dated from the past reached out to me and wanted to have lunch. She had been thinking of me and wanted to see where it would go. Although she is awesome, we still were not a connection romantically. A few days later, another person from my past reached out and wanted to have dinner. When that didn't work out, a mutual acquaintance randomly reached out to me on Instagram and wanted to set me up with her friend.

It is that random message from Instagram I received who I am currently dating. She is awesome and I have yet to find any red flags. The point is when we are not looking for a woman, when we are not trying to find a date, they just show up. It's like when we are single, we can't find any single women. When we are dating, single women are everywhere.

As mentioned in the friends section of this book, when we think of dating, we should start off as friends. When I connect with a woman on a dating app, I almost always say, "If it doesn't work out, at least I will have made a friend." I mean that. Everyone out there is interesting and can add value to our life.

Outside the dating apps, we want to look at Meetup groups; joining things that interest us will be a way to meet women who like the same things as we do. It's not forced. We are both at the basket-weaving event because we want to be. She didn't make us go to the event, and we didn't make her come to the event; therefore, we have a mutual interest already.

My favorite, although I've never met anyone romantically, is Toastmasters; this is where we will find some high energy people who want to succeed in life. They are individuals who want more in their lives than sitting on their hands and not living to the fullest. I will always recommend Toastmasters for just about any scenario we have in life, so just join!

There is always our place of worship. Not just going to services but getting involved in the fundraising or social events they have. Do they have outreach activities? Are there committees we can join to help our community or parish? Can we lead a youth group, teach Sunday school, or lead a Bible study group? If that sounds too scary, we know what to do; it's one word: Toastmasters.

Rotary clubs are a great place to meet professionals who like to give back to the community; they are involved in fundraising and a lot of volunteering. I have done some presentations at Rotary clubs, and they have a mix of all types of people. Before speaking at Rotary, I had a perception of what types of people I would encounter there. I was wrong. There are all types of interesting people, and we should maybe take a peek into one of their 35,000 clubs.

Go back to night school to complete an education or learn a new skill. Other like-minded people are there. We shouldn't just go to meet someone; we should go as part of our continual growth in our lives. Continual learning keeps us interesting and gives us new outlooks on life.

And of course, our friends. Don't ask them to set us up. Eventually they will want to set us up because we are an awesome guy for someone they know. Like the woman on Instagram. I don't really know her; I know her through a Meetup group. We never talked one-on-one; we spoke only a few times in a group setting. We followed each other on Instagram and Facebook. She saw what I was doing, knew the type of person I am, and decided I would be worthy of meeting her friend. It was a big compliment that someone who doesn't really know me wanted to set me up with one of her close friends. I believe that says something positive about me. Again, it's about that continual growth in life.

We are not going to meet anyone sitting in our living room, we will need to get out there and do something. Do something we have always been interested in doing or have not yet tried. Go do it. Who knows? We might find the perfect person going through the same journey.

CHAPTER 6

Exercise

Why do we need to exercise?

We just covered dating, and now it's time to get back into shape and get ready for that first date. Why do we need to exercise anyway? Is there more to it than getting muscles and looking fit? The first reason is it's how we can lose weight, along with a proper diet. (Yuck. We'll talk about this is a later chapter.) To build and maintain muscle, the body has to burn fat. Exercise not only helps us lose weight, but it also helps prevent weight gain. The more we exercise, the more calories we burn, and the more weight we lose. My stepfather is a doctor and from a teenager on, he always told me the same formula: burn more calories than you consume. It's such a simple solution but obviously a difficult concept for us all to follow.

Second, it helps lower the risk of some diseases and helps decrease developing conditions, such as obesity, type 2 diabetes, high blood pressure, strokes, depression, and anxiety. How does exercise help with diseases and mainly heart disease? When we exercise, we increase our high-density lipoprotein cholesterol, which is referred to as HDL. This is considered the good cholesterol, which helps decrease the bad cholesterol called triglycerides. No, I'm not that smart. I obtained this information from the Mayo Clinic.

Third, it improves our endurance (a.k.a. lasting longer in bed). Do I need to continue, or is that a good enough reason? Lasting longer, doing more, ability to maneuver her in different positions and scenarios. Maybe this should have been the first reason and just left it with that. In reality though, over time, we do get too tired to have sex, or get too exhausted before we finish. Exercise will not only increase our energy levels, but it will make us feel better about ourselves. When we feel better about ourselves, we are more likely to ask a woman out of a date or try new things.

Fourth, when we exercise, our body delivers oxygen and nutrients to our tissues to help the cardiovascular system work better. This gives us more energy for our normal daily activities, not to mention item number three above.

Fifth, one of the main reasons I started exercising after my separation was to change my mood. There were some very stressful, depressing, and challenging times; a good walk or workout would help change those emotions. Exercise helps stimulate various brain chemicals that will help us relax and have less anxiety. As we continue to work out, we will notice a difference in our physique, and we will have higher self-esteem when we have to use the next notch to the left on our belt to tighten our pants up.

Other benefits include helping our memory and brain function. If we have worked out enough, we know it helps with our sleep. Regular exercise will help us fall asleep faster and help us get a better, deeper sleep. Plus throw in some melatonin and we will be having a restful night.

Any form of exercise burns more calories than sitting on the couch. Any exercise is better than none, no matter how little. If it's been a while, start off slow and take bigger steps each time; do it at our own pace, but do it on a regular basis. Be consistent.

Think Outside the Box (a.k.a. the Gym)

After my separation, I did the logical thing. I joined the gym. I was going to get into awesome shape, have all of the ladies I wanted, in fact my pulsating biceps would be so irresistible that women would fawn over me at the gym and I wouldn't have to worry about dating apps. Yeah, that didn't happen.

I did the thing almost daily for four-plus years. Came in, hit the treadmill for a half hour, lifted some weights, did some ab exercises, hit the tanning bed, then went home. Every day, every week, every month, every year! Same boring routine, and I never met anyone. I just had others around me doing the same exact thing, year after year. I noticed those same people after several years; they didn't look to have had any improvements either. They were wearing the same T-shirt, same beer belly, the gym wasn't doing it for them, nor for me; I think my body was nearly identical before and after working out for four years.

I saw the club trainer around for a few years as well. One day it was slow, he came over, gave me some tips, and we had a light conversation. I decided to work with the trainer for a few sessions; it was free at this club. Our first session, we did some interesting exercises, using mostly resistance bands and a couple of dumbbells. Second session, same thing. I asked him, "With all of the equipment in the gym, why are we not using the weights or equipment provided?" He said we don't need that stuff. His quote was "Does a monkey need to lift weights to climb a tree?" His point was we just do what our body needs us to do for our regular daily activities. We don't need to bench-press three hundred pounds to pick up a cup of coffee or drive to work. Doing pushups is just as effective as bench-pressing an overabundance of weight.

Within a week, I quit the gym. What the heck was I doing there? I started looking for alternatives; the first thing I did was buy a Body Boss, which is a home resistance set. I enjoy this compact device; it is a home gym that I still use, and I believe it was around $200. Then I started walking, mountain biking, hiking, rock climbing, paddleboarding, and going to ropes courses at the US Whitewater Center near my home. I believe the rock climbing and ropes courses are some of the best exercises for me, it's not lifting weights, it's using our own weight in a controlled effort to create a result.

My point is there is nothing wrong with going to the gym and pumping iron to sculpt our muscles. If that is our thing, enjoy. However, if we go to the gym because we believe it's the only alternative, then read on, my friend, because there are plenty of opportunities to exercise. There are ways to be healthy, breathe fresh air, and talk to people outside the gym. Being stuck in a gym for four years made me realize how easily COVID-19 could have been created in there. It's a petri dish of germs. We have the sweaty equipment that people don't wipe down after usage, the farting, the burping, the body odor, the grunting, etc. How did I survive in there? Get outside and do things.

As I mentioned in the making friends chapter, we want to check out the Meetup app. It is available in our phone's app store. We can find ample things to do for exercise, such as hiking, biking, rock climbing, dragon boat racing, kayaking, walking, dodge ball, and softball. All sports are on there. Get out, do something different, breathe fresh air, and meet like-minded people while we stay in shape and feel good about ourselves.

If there is an REI in the area, they have a lot of great opportunities for us to step out of your comfort zone and try some different things. Check out Rei.com/events in the local area. Their cost is a little more, but they provide an instructor, usually gear needed for the activity, and get a group of people who are paying and will take it a little more seriously. The REI near me has guided kayaking trips, biking, hiking, backcountry navigation, camping, rafting, stewardship, and traveling adventures to other destinations. This goes to the things we want to do: exercise, meet new people, make friends or romantic interest, learn new skills, step out of our comfort zone, and maybe find our passion.

It was my life coach who introduced me to hiking, rock climbing, and camping. Hiking and camping have become my passion; I like camping with a group of friends but am very comfortable hiking out on the trail seven to ten miles solo and camping out in the middle of nowhere. I've got a passion for camping and hiking now. I'm looking to hike the Appalachian Trail in the near future, 2,190 miles from Georgia to Maine. I never would have discovered this passion if I hadn't taken that first step and gone hiking and camping, even though I was reluctant to do so.

Social Benefits of Exercise

When I've talked of exercise, it's usually a reference to a group activity, a way to connect and meet with other like-minded people, and a way to have a group of people to interact with. And I'm talking about a sport that we are engaged in; sitting at the ball game does not count as exercise, although some of those stadiums can add quite a few steps and stairs to our exercise smartwatch. There are some social benefits to exercising and doing activities with others.

It helps build relationships; we meet people who are interested in doing the same things we are doing. Usually, an activity or sport requires we work together as a team; we learn the strengths and weaknesses of others, and they discover our strengths and weaknesses. We learn to work together based on that learned knowledge and can use those skills during future events. We can also use this information and these team-building exercises to determine if we are compatible friends or have a possible romantic connection.

We tend to have a good attitude when we show up to meet new people. If we continue an activity week after week, we look forward to it and our attitude continues to get better when we get closer to the gathering. We then think of how we can improve ourselves to be better and make the experience more enjoyable for others. Maybe our joyful glee will have us bringing the group coffee first thing in the morning or snacks. When my tribe and I would go for a day hike, we usually went to a waterfall during the colder months so we could do a polar plunge. I would take my backpack, some camp cooking gear, as well as hot cocoa, marshmallows, tea, and disposable cups for the treat. It became our thing; whenever we would make it to the destination, we would have a nice warm treat. And yes, I would carry the empty paper coffee cups and lids out in a bag and throw them away later.

With others looking forward to our participation and relying on us, we become more accountable and reliable. If they need us for an activity, we don't show up, and therefore the activity cannot be done, we are not a reliable participant. Our lack of dependability affects the enjoyment of others. When we would go rock climbing on a mountain, my life coach has half the gear and I had half of the gear; therefore, we'd both need to show up to make it happen for the group. She has the rope, but I have the harness. We can't rock climb with one and not the other. Our activity becomes about others and we look forward to helping out and contributing.

When we join these activities, someone usually has the knowledge and experience on how to do it. They will help us learn the skills needed to be a team player as well as teach us how to do it and enjoy our time doing it. They will teach us the proper way to do things, not only the activity itself but also the setup and takedown of any equipment or procedures needed. Back to my first camping experience and hiking on the Appalachian Trail, there was an experienced bushman along with us; that poor guy, I must have asked him one hundred questions. I was interested, he was my only reference point, and I think he enjoyed being a mentor sharing his knowledge with others.

This new group of like-minded friends become our peer group for that activity. They will help and encourage us to do better and learn. They will raise our standards and give us a competitive edge. We all have our thing, our strengths. When we go rock climbing as a group, I make it about halfway up the side of the mountain, and that's enough for me, I get a little tired and my nerves get the better of me as I climb higher and higher.

Others make it a goal to make it to the top, and when they do, we all celebrate for them. I enjoy rock climbing; I know making it to the top would give me a sense of accomplishment, but I don't make it a must. Plus I'm the oldest dude in the group; everyone else has different abilities than I do. When we go camping, I'm the go-to guy. I have the knowledge, passion, and experience to make it enjoyable for others.

Based on the activity we are doing, we more than likely have similar fitness goals with the others in the group. This is another form of a support group to encourage each other, give each other tips on diet and exercise, and hopefully, we will hold each other accountable. We will then develop some discipline to meet those fitness goals not only for ourselves, but for the others when they see us week after week, they will notice the change (Thomas, 2021).

Make better choices; be alert to the little things that can help with our health. For instance, I have a two-story house; the master bathroom is upstairs at the far end of the home. Additionally, there is a half bath downstairs next to the kitchen. When I am downstairs and need to use the bathroom, I always go up to the master bath. This requires me to take the stairs and get in a few more steps. It's not a lot, but doing it three to five times a day adds up.

Parking a little farther away from the store or office increases the number of steps and exercise we receive. I would always giggle at the gym when I'd see people waiting to park in the first few spaces closest to the front doors. Maybe they wanted to conserve their energy for the gym?

Another great device is my Apple Watch. Every hour it reminds me to get up and move. I love it! Sometimes we get involved in our work, or we are sitting on the sofa watching a movie and forget to move. Even on longer Zoom meetings it will remind me to stand and move around. I turn off my camera and do just that.

Exercise is an important part of our physical and mental health. Find what you enjoy and do it. It doesn't have to be just one thing, but it has to be something.

A word of caution. As we try new activities, we get involved in them and make them our passion. As we are single guys who may want to date someone else, make sure this new hobby is not your only gig. Many of my dates would ask me what else I do, other than hiking, camping, and rock climbing. Well, not much of anything; that is what I enjoy doing. Some women enjoy a play, opera, the theater, a concert, bowling, golf, etc. If we become a one-trick pony, we may miss out on a wonderful woman but also other activities and cultural awakenings.

Chapter 7

Self-Care

We talked about dating, we talked about getting ourselves in shape, now let's talk about self-care—doing the extra stuff that is a bonus. Self-care helps us relax, focus on us, and allow our daily stressors to melt away. When we talk about self-care, we aren't talking about being selfish; we're talking about doing things for ourselves that will benefit our health and well-being.

Massage

Massage, from a legitimate establishment. I love massage. I usually doze off for a little bit while the therapist is working on me. It is a simple pleasure, it's relaxing, and it has health benefits. There have been times when I have a pinched nerve or soreness and the massage therapist works on it and makes it all better! Now while she's working on it, it doesn't feel better, but later it does.

Massage also helps with your body's circulation and overall body functions through proper stretching and movement of parts of your body you usually can't attend to on your own. I am a member of Massage Envy. I pay a fairly low monthly fee that enables me to get one sixty-minute massage; I usually pay extra and go for the ninety minutes, and usually twice a month. There is a discount as a member for the longer massage sessions.

I like to go with whomever is available; I like variety, especially with a massage. Each therapist is different; they all have the same routines and parts of the body they work on, but each one seems to do things a little differently. I'm always amazed when it feels like a totally different massage because this person does something different from the last person, and so on. Some therapists kick my butt. I'll leave exhausted because of the manipulation of my body, but for the next few weeks, I feel great! Other times I leave totally relaxed. I'm happy either way. It's variety and it's beneficial to our body.

Skin Care

For the past almost thirty years, I have given myself facials, done scrubs, used moisturizers, and used those nose strips to keep the blackheads away. This all started because when I was younger, much better-looking, in shape, and full of myself, a girl pointed out I had blackheads. I didn't know what they were, but I knew it was a flaw. I wasn't having it; I needed to eliminate them.

Fast-forward to today. I have been to places to get facials and they had little or nothing to do; they would all say I take care of my skin and they felt as if I made their job easy. Facials refresh your skin, pull out the blackheads, remove dead skin, and help clear clogged pours. I'm a bit of an overachiever on facials; I have one of those facial steamers to open my pours. I then use the clay, charcoal, or seaweed facial products found in most drugstores. I use facial cream for the day that includes a PDF and a night face cream to moisturize my face and help with the signs of aging. When we look our best, we feel our best.

As mentioned, I use face moisturizers daily. In fact, it feels odd when I don't use them. If I am driving and realize I didn't put on moisturizer, I'll stop at the first drugstore I see to buy some instead of waiting to get home later in the day. Moisturizers come in a variety of types. Just start using one; over time, we will find what works best for us. Each day we put it off is a little more time for our skin to deteriorate. It's never too late to start taking care of our skin. Why not start today if we haven't in the past?

On average, the moisturizers I buy are $20 to $30, and I do like to try different types. I don't have one that is my favorite. I like to sample different formulas. Yes, I have bought $200 moisturizers, and no, I saw zero difference between the high-priced one and the low-priced one. And I know we are all macho men; the person who really got me into face moisturizers was a contractor friend of mine who did drywall and ceilings. He's a typical blue-collar worker driving a van, but he has a bottle of moisturizer in the vehicle that he puts on daily.

Meditation

Meditation is one I try again and again and fail every time. I either fall asleep or I'm thinking of something else. But I will talk about it briefly because I know it is beneficial, and maybe one of these days I'll actually be able to meditate and get to a higher level. Meditation helps us clear our mind in order to focus on nothing. Once we get to the nothing stage, we can relax. The answers, solutions, or ideas we are seeking will come to us during those peaceful moments.

We can also meditate just to meditate; we don't have to seek answers or guidance. We can just relax our body and mind, so we have minimal stimulus going on. Meditation allows us to be present in the here and now. Taking time to meditate requires us to make the time to chill out, to just sit quietly and do nothing for fifteen minutes to an hour. It takes discipline.

Since I started writing this book, I have got into meditation a little bit. It's my form of meditation. When I'm hiking for five to twelve miles, I don't listen to music; I'm usually alone, lost in my thoughts. What I do is try to eliminate the noise in my head and focus on the trees, the trail, the sky, my breathing. If I start to think of work, I will focus on an object, usually a tree, and just think about that in order to get work out of my mind. If I start thinking of dinner or the Yankees game, I again focus on something as I hike to eliminate those distracting thoughts from my mind. I don't know if that's real meditation, but it's my meditation.

Yoga

Yoga is another item I'm not into; however, I have recently started stretching and doing some yogalike moves at home. I'm not a limber person, and part of the training to hike the Appalachian Trail is to be limber and in the best shape I can be. I can see myself getting into yoga in the near future; I just haven't done so yet. I put yoga in this chapter versus the exercise chapter because yoga is more than exercise, although most people I see who do yoga are in great shape.

Like meditation, yoga helps us relax, calm down, and decrease our breathing and heart rate. It obviously increases our strength and physique as well as gets us limber and flexible. It helps with our balance; have you ever seen some of those poses? If I'm going to be hiking for 2,190 with a thirty- to thirty-five-pound backpack, I could use some balance! Yoga can help with back pain; I do a few poses to stretch out and strengthen my back. I don't have back pain, but I want to keep it that way, so I do stretch out.

And back to previous chapters, yoga is a good place to meet people as well as exercise in various environments. Many are outdoors so we can breathe, enjoy nature, and exercise. We need to have focus on our thoughts and our body. I'm pro yoga. I just don't do it yet.

Hot Bath

When I started this book, I didn't have baths included because I've always had showers or one of those small generic bathtubs. My new house has one of those larger Roman tubs so I can actually take a bath. When I think of bubble baths, I think of my grandkids playing in them; however, it's an adult thing too.

One of my massage therapists recommended taking a hot bath with Epsom salt to help relax sore muscles, especially for my legs after a good workout. There used to be one generic type of Epsom salt; however, there are now a variety of formulas I enjoy, including lavender or eucalyptus and spearmint, even coconut. Why Epsom salt? Because it contains magnesium and as we soak, it helps our body get rid of toxins. The magnesium helps reduce stiffness or swelling from working out. Epsom salts do not dissolve in cold water; therefore, you need to use a nice, hot bath with them.

Yes, I even take the occasional bubble bath. Remember that Mr. Bubble brand? I use that when I can find it, but again, I like variety. They have those bath bombs now where you put them in the tub and they start to fizz up, change the color of the water, or add lots of bubbles. Here's a tip that I found on vacation: if we are in a nice place with a jacuzzi tub, use a bath bomb. The jacuzzi circulating the water and soap products will create a ginormous number of bubbles that most kids would be envious of!

Cold Shower

Cold showers help the circulation in our body. As we know, when cold water hits our body, it reacts very differently and immediately. The cold water causes the blood in our body, specifically our tissues, to get moving quicker in order to get the body to a proper temperature. This is something I'm working on doing; I do try to turn it down as cold as possible as I am completing my shower, but it is difficult. My tribe and I will do polar plunges at waterfalls or in rivers along a hiking trail in the winter. Those offer the same benefits, but we do it more as a thrill or challenge.

Other benefits of a cold shower include changing our mood to a positive one; I can attest to that as I'm always laughing at myself as I try to stand there in a freezing shower. It speeds up our body's metabolism. Obviously it starts working harder to try to warm you up as mentioned above about your circulation.

I also do this type of exercise during cold months where I take the dog for a walk. I don't bundle up as much as I should; therefore, my body is trying to warm me up, which increases my metabolism and burns calories. A cold shower also energizes us. If we have ever taken one, we know as we get out of the shower we are saying, "Oh my God! Oh my God!" We are all hyped up. Finally, we will save money on our hot water bill.

Shaving

I have a full beard and choose to shave every day. I shave my neck and cheek areas to keep things looking clean and orderly. Everyone has their own style, but for me, having a full beard, trimmed, groomed, and clean cut, seems to be my preference. The women I know and associate with prefer men with a groomed beard. I also know women who don't like facial hair; I'm not going out with them.

Based on my body size, a beard works best for me; it actually makes me look thinner. Even when I've lost weight, I'll shave off the beard and be horrified by who I see in the mirror. A beard seems to be my thing. If we haven't tried to grow one, do it. We might like it. I had a goatee for a long time, but so did everyone else. Once I grew in a beard, it was part of who I am. Changing who we are could include growing a beard or shaving one off. It goes along with a different hairstyle, glasses, new clothing, etc.; it's all about change.

I do shave daily, again my neck and cheeks because I do want to look clean, even with a beard. It also shows I am grooming on a regular basis and take care of myself. It is just part of a routine of being the best I can, even something as simple as shaving.

Breathing

Breathing we take for granted, but if done properly, it can increase the overall function of our body. Tony Robbins talked about how when some of us are stressed, we pick up a cigarette; we take a deep breath in and then exhale the smoke. Doing it over and over as we smoke our cigarette calms us down. Tony went on to say to try the same exercise without the cigarette. Just do some deep breathing.

A number of my friends follow and practice Wim Hoff, who provides breathing exercises. I do some of the techniques and do feel a difference. I cannot properly explain Wim Hoff Breathing; therefore, I am providing a link to see if this is something of interest: https://www.wimhofmethod.com/breathing-exercises.

For several years now, I have been a hiker doing long-distance and strenuous hikes. In the past, I would just huff and puff mile after mile. Inevitably I would have to stop and catch my breath. Since I started studying proper breathing exercises, I can now focus on my breath as I hike. When the trail gets difficult, I focus on my breath, making sure it is slowed down a bit and has a proper pace. My mind doesn't think about anything other than my breathing. It seems to help me hike more efficiently, and I'm not huffing and puffing, just breathing normal breaths.

Nature

Speaking of hiking, getting out into nature is a relaxing activity we should do wherever we are. It can be the beach, the forest, a neighborhood trail, the mountains, or the valley. When we are in nature, we are breathing fresh air, most likely exercising, and hopefully disconnecting from our electronics. Where I go, there tends to be little or no phone service.

When we are doing activities outdoors and are present with what we are doing, we feel connected to nature. It calms us, we tend to feel better emotionally, and it contributes to our well-being. It is hard to be stressed out when we are walking through a forest with nothing but the noises of nature.

Once we get into nature and enjoy the benefits, it becomes addicting. One of my favorite quotes is by John Muir. "The mountains are calling, and I must go." It is so true! When I don't get out into nature, I get a little stir crazy. Lately I've been busy finishing this book and moving into my new house. I've had to resort to hiking along the miles of concrete sidewalks in my neighborhood. It's nice to be able to do so; however, I need to get back into nature. I need to get back to the mountains. They are calling!

Essential Oils

I use essential oils in my home; I have a couple of diffusers that I add water and oils to. They create a pleasant smell in the home. I use essential oils for a couple of reasons. The first reason is because I have heard that candles and incense can be bad for us as they can have toxic chemicals that are released into the air, and we breathe those toxins in.

I've read a number of different articles and have spoken to different experts, and there is no conclusive evidence that candles are as bad as they are made out to be. Most candles are made from paraffin wax, which is a petroleum product; petroleum is what gasoline is made from. The amount of toxins that come out of candles is minimal and it hasn't been shown to create health issues. The wick that we light and blow out does create some toxic smoke. Therefore, when we blow them out, don't stand next to them or breathe in the air; maybe open a window and/ or put on a fan.

Another concern I've heard about is that scented candles have formaldehyde, which is a cancer risk. They do have some levels of formaldehyde; however, it again seems to be minimal, and unless we are standing over the candle breathing, it doesn't seem to be a concern. All of these concerns are why I went to essential oils! If we have concerns, try beeswax, soy wax, or palm wax candles. They are a little pricier, but they don't have that petroleum concern in them.

Back to the essential oils. They are made from compounds extracted from plants. As with any product on the market, make sure we are getting quality oils that will cost a little more. But with everything, we get what we pay for.

The essential oils make the house smell good. I have different scents as I change them daily, and it just creates a nice ambiance, especially if the diffuser lights up. Essential oils are said to reduce stress as an aromatherapy type application. Orange is an anxiety reducing oil; it has a nice smell and is a relaxing scent. Tea tree oils I use on my feet. I hike often and far, and tea tree oil help with athlete's foot and related issues. I was reading some Appalachian Trail through-hiker books, and they mention using tea tree oil on their feet along their 2,190-mile journey.

Sleep benefits come from using lavender oil; we can use it in our diffuser to help us fall asleep. I have firsthand experience with the lavender oil. I decided to put a diffuser in my home office, which obviously has a smaller space than the living room. I was using lavender for a few days in the office and found myself falling asleep during the day as I worked! I got rid of the lavender diffuser and was able to work. The point is it does help you fall asleep.

Sleep

Sleep is a priority for all we do; a lack of sleep is more than bags and dark circles under our eyes. Adults are supposed to get seven to nine hours of sleep a night. I'm at six to seven with seven being the maximum; my body/mind just won't let me sleep in late. Eight o'clock in the morning is sleeping in really late for me. I'm usually up by six thirty to seven o'clock and haven't used an alarm clock in years. When I do set one for a flight or important meeting, I will literally wake up five to ten minutes before the alarm goes off. It's odd! Experts say it's an internal body clock. Mine goes off each morning.

A lack of sleep creates low energy throughout the day as we try to work through being tired. We don't concentrate as much at our activities and are slower to react in situations like driving. A lack of sleep also makes us moody; how many times have we said, "I'm tired" when people are trying to get our attention? It seems as if the only time our phone rings or buzzes is when we are trying to get in a quick nap. True story: I have a good relationship with my CEO; we chat once a month or every other month to catch up. One day I was taking a nap during company time (I work remotely) and she called. My CEO woke me up to say hello! I didn't tell her I was sleeping.

In our next chapter, we address erectile disfunction; one of the contributing factors to that is a lack of sleep. Do we usually wake up with wood or a few hours after nodding off we are good to go? That's because we have rested, cleared our mind; our body and mind are operating properly. When we are tired, we don't perform as well, if at all. One of the reasons we don't sleep well is because of stress. We'll deal with these issues in the next chapter.

Some tips for a good night's sleep include making sure we have black-out curtains in our room. When it's dark, our body starts to release melatonin that makes us become tired. I take melatonin supplements to help me fall asleep quickly, but when I've had a good day exercising, I usually won't take them and let myself fall asleep naturally. Today I did a ten-mile hike in the sun. I should pass out as soon as I hit the pillow.

Skip dessert: Sugar in the evening will make it difficult to sleep. Coffee, soda, sweet tea, energy drinks—all of these items will keep us awake if we drink them late in the afternoon. The other night I was lying wide-awake at two in the morning, and I started thinking of what I consumed that was keeping me awake. Around seven thirty I had a big jug of Gatorade. I Googled it, and yes, it has sugar in it.

One of the main reasons we don't sleep well is stress. We have way too much on our mind; we are thinking of every problem and issue we have. Motivational guru Earl Nightingale had a simple technique to help eliminate stress. Whatever our problem is, take a legal pad, write out the problem, and then do some brainstorming on ways to tackle that problem. Revisit the list the next day, and the day after that as needed, but now the problem is out of our mind and is sitting on a piece of paper waiting for it to be resolved.

Part of our stress is trying to remember all of the things we need to do, a speech we need to give, or an idea we have; get that legal pad, write it down, and now, our mind can rest. An added benefit is once we write things down, our mind doesn't need to try to remember that information. It is on paper; now our mind can be free to start thinking of solutions and other things.

My final tip or trick for sleeping is a sound machine. Being with my grandkids and falling asleep with them got me used to their sound machine that consists of white noise. I have an Alexa next to the bed and she plays either ocean sounds or white noise. This drowns out the outside noises as well as has this rhythm to help us sleeping. I've been doing this for years, and I believe it's like Pavlov's dog. My body knows when it hears the white noise that it's time to fall asleep. Now that I've been sleeping at my girlfriend's house, I have an app on my phone for the white noise as her house is very quiet.

Journaling

Yes, journaling is like keeping a diary. Journaling is a way to put down our thoughts, what's going on in our life, and our expectations. As mentioned above, once we put our thoughts on paper, we clear our mind and come up with new ideas. Journaling is something we can go back to and see where we were six months ago or a year ago versus where we are now. We can see the growth we've made over time.

We should do a daily journal for about twenty minutes. Based on writing books, coaching, and speeches, I am doing a form of journaling daily. On a monthly basis, I do write a letter to myself and date it. This letter is about where I am financially—the decisions I've made regarding my finances and large purchases. I will usually have a plan on how to pay off those larger purchases. I will include investments and goals financially. I do like to review it each month to see where I'm at and update it as needed.

We can't know where we are going if we don't know where we have been. Journaling and reviewing our journal will help us with that process. It's like kids. We see them all the time so we don't see their growth. A friend who hasn't seen them in a while will say, "Wow, the kids have really grown!" This is going to be the same with us. As we start to rebuild our life, we might not see the growth, but if we've done a journal, we can go back and notice the incremental changes we've made.

David Jones

Medical

Getting an annual physical and checkup is an important part of our self-care and well-being. By visiting a doctor annually, we can know where we are at; are there any issues we can work on before they become life threatening? We won't know what is going on inside our body without checking in with our doctor and allowing a number of tests and exams to determine our overall health.

Dentist and eye doctor appointments are essential as well; I go to my semiannual dental appointment and it is just part of the process of doing what we have to do. Plus I pay for my medical insurance; therefore, I want to get my money's worth. Consider going to specialists as well, specifically a dermatologist to check us out with a full body scan to make sure we don't have skin cancer or issues in areas that we can't see.

Gratitude

Gratitude is being thankful for what we have in our life, what we have done in our life. It's the opposite of being envious of others or wishing we had something we don't currently have. The purpose of gratitude is to shift our focus from what we do not have to what we have. When we realize what we have in our life, it gives us power and appreciation. It's the possessions we currently have, the people we have in our life, the experiences we have had thus far. Have the focus of all that is good in our life; when we start listing things, journaling items, people, and events, we realize how fortunate we are.

Gratitude is not just being thankful for what we have; it is expecting and being grateful for what we want to happen. At night, most do their gratitude before they go to sleep; they say all the things they are thankful for. In the morning, they do expectation gratitude where they express the type of day they are expecting to have: a sales call they want to go well, a presentation that will be a hit, etc. We put that thought out there the day we want to have it; however, we have to precede it with the skills and preparedness to make it happen.

In the book, movie, and program called *The Secret,* the concept is to tell the universe what we want, and we will attract it into our life. That was the premise for a long time. Many of us did that and things did not come into our lives that we asked the universe for. The program followed up with a new movie that indicated we have to do more than tell the universe what we want; we need to do the hard work, prepare, and perfect our craft. Once we have all of the technical and mental skills needed to attract those things into our life, those items will come into our life.

We live in a period of uncertainty; however, we as humans like certainty. We have uncertainty with politics, the stock market, our jobs, our debit, COVID-19, Bitcoin, and a number of other events. With such uncertainty, we have anxiety and a decrease in our peace of mind. We are emotionally exhausted with all that is going wrong and what can go wrong.

With gratitude, we focus on what is going right, what has gone right, and we project what we expect to go right in the future. We take control, focus on the positive, and block out the noise of the negative. If we focus on all that is good in our life, those circumstance that aren't good won't shake us as much; we have a base of good things in our life: our accomplishments and such.

David Jones

Make Your Bed

US Navy Admiral William H. McRaven said, "Make your bed, if you make your bed each morning, you will have completed the first task of the day." He went on to say, "If you can't do the little things, you can't do the big things." I've made my bed my entire life. Thinking back as far as I can, my mom always had me do so. While married and then when I was single, I've always made my bed. It's just something I've always done. Then hearing this speech by the admiral, it made sense as to why I do it. At the end of the day, it's like arriving at a hotel, a well-made bed waiting for me to fold down the sheet and climb into.

Gardening

I have a deck at the back of my house where I have a container garden. I have a variety of pots, buckets, and an old recycle bin where I grow a variety of plants. I have tomatoes, cucumbers, strawberries, hot peppers, and an array of herbs growing. Of course, my pride and joy is my three-year-old: my lemon tree that I grew from a seed. It's now twelve feet tall. I bring it inside during the winter as lemon trees don't do well below freezing.

I hate to admit this, but when it was just a one-year-old baby tree, I went to Orlando, Florida, to visit my younger daughter; I put the dog in the kennel and the tree in my car for the drive down. Once at the hotel, which had a screened in patio, I let it bask in the Florida weather for a few days.

Having fresh vegies and herbs in the backyard is a way to relive stress. Each morning I go out and water them, then I check for ripe fruits and vegetables as well as bugs who might be hanging out on the leaves. I will use a sprayer with soap water to spray the plants and deter the bugs.

It is my morning ritual, and each year I'm happy with how large my small container garden gets. It brings me joy, and it's time I make first thing in the morning to breathing in fresh air and tend to the plants. It's my self-care, my well-being. Even the smallest of gardens can do the same for us.

Self-care is about us. It is the way we treat ourselves. Since we should now love ourselves, based on a previous chapter, we realize we deserve to do things just for ourselves. Focus on our needs; that could be physical, mental, spiritual, or just the need to relax and do any number of the items above.

CHAPTER 8

Erectile Dysfunction

ED affects 40 percent of men over the age of forty. There are an estimated 30 million men in the United States dealing with erectile dysfunction and 100 million men worldwide. We are not alone! This chapter and all other chapters are to let us know we are not alone! What we are going through is life is unique to each one of us; however, on a broad stroke, we all have the same issues, and the goal is to talk about it.

Once again, I'm not a medical professional and cannot render medical advice or speak as an authority. What I will do is give my perspective and experiences as this book is about my personal journey and hoping it helps along our journey.

Talking about ED is a difficult subject; it is even difficult to talk to our doctors about it. I had a urologist a few years ago. It was my first time to the office, and I didn't realize the doctor was a woman—an attractive younger woman. Worse yet, the assistant who came in before the doctor seemed like a young Swedish supermodel, and I had to explain to her why I was there to see the doctor. I was polite, spoke to the doctor, but left to never go back; it was just too comfortable for me.

A breakthrough for talking openly about ED came from a random person. My day job is in the workers compensation insurance business. I was visiting with a new policyholder at his home office; he was a construction contractor. We were about the same age, but he was in great shape—a very muscular and confident guy. We hit it off and talked for a while about business and life. I asked about his workout routine and it was similar to mine, but he was in such better shape. He asked if I had my testosterone tested. I didn't even know what that was.

He told me as we get older, our bodies produce less testosterone. Testosterone is not just what helps us with sex; it also helps with weight loss, building muscle, and having our bodies function properly. He told me he did his own injections once a week; in fact, it was injection time for him the day of my visit. He said he'd show me how easy it is. He went and got his prescribed vile of testosterone and a needle, and wearing shorts, he showed me how he just injected it into his thigh. Looked easy enough. We had a great talk about testosterone, sex, Viagra, woman, etc. It was refreshing to be able to openly talk to someone about the subject. This is something I wouldn't talk to any of my friends or family about.

When I visited the doctor and got my testosterone test, I was in the three hundreds; no wonder I wasn't losing weight, gaining muscle, had low energy, and a low sex drive. On average, we should be between three hundred and one thousand nanograms of testosterone from a blood test. Forty percent of men over forty-five have less than three hundred, hence the need for testosterone in most of our systems. Once I got my testosterone and started doing my own injections, I was up near one thousand.

David Jones

Self-administering the shots into your leg or butt is not that difficult; after the first time, it's easy.

I started my testosterone journey at one of those franchise men's clinics. They were very expensive and did some procedures that were supposed to make me eighteen again, which didn't work. I'm glad I experienced them just to know what's out there and gain an education—an education for me as to what not to do. At first, I was a baby and didn't want to do the shots in the leg every week. This clinic had some testosterone pellets they put inside your back side and over time they released the testosterone into your body. They did an incision in my butt cheek, inserted six to ten pellets that look and felt like gel caps you take for medicine. I liked it because I only had to do it every six months.

Unfortunately, I had a bad experience with the pellets; I spoke to a couple of other guys who also had the same experience as I did. Since we sit on our butt all the time, at work, at home, and as we drive, the pellets were being pushed up toward the incision. Eventually, the pressure opened the incision and they started to come out. As you can imagine, this freaked me out. Reaching back there and feeling something popping out of my skin was not normal.

I went back to the clinic and they reclosed the incision. When they do the initial incision, they numb you with some shots so you don't feel it. They don't sew you up though, they just use a butterfly bandage, which I though was odd. Eventually, another pellet popped out, but this time I knew what was going on so I was able to bandage myself up. I felt as if I was getting ripped off because I was now missing two pellets of testosterone; however, the clinic told me they put extra in at the start with the anticipation this happens. That would have been good to know from the onset.

Six months later, it was time to do it again; unfortunately, they didn't inject enough numbing solution into my tushy. At one point as they were stuffing the pellets into the fat of my butt, I felt it very distinctly; it is an awful feeling. They numbed me again and finished the procedure. I was a little traumatized from that experience and knew I would never do it again; it is a feeling you don't forget. Second round, I again had a pellet come out, which of course is not a pleasant experience either. For me, I'm not a pellet guy.

Six months later, same clinic. I don't know why I went back after those experiences, but I did. This time I got the self-administered injections into my thigh. That worked out well, and overall, I was happy with the results. In fact I did it for two years.

Then COVID-19 hit, and I got a little ticked off at them because I felt I was getting ripped off. The clinic has a pharmacy send the vial of testosterone by UPS; we have to wait until we are out of our last vial before we can order more. No, we cannot order it before we run out. They know when we should be due. Therefore, we usually miss a shot, or it might be delayed a few days. When COVID-19 hit, the pharmacies were delayed in filling orders; there was a two- to three-week wait time, which means I didn't have a shot for several weeks at a time.

It didn't hurt the pharmacy, it didn't hurt the clinic, but it hurt me financially because we buy a one-year plan. I estimate during COVID-19, I received ten months of testosterone instead of twelve months. I don't like being taken advantage of or losing money, so I moved on from that organization.

I now get my testosterone from my doctor who prescribes it; part of it is covered by my insurance, so it is much more cost effective. My advice therefore is to go to our doctor or our urologist and get the self-administered shots. There are some companies I found on Instagram and Facebook who send us a kit; we send them some blood samples from our finger, and then we can get our self-administered shots from them. I got four kits (paid for two); all of them had a problem or issue even though I followed the directions perfectly. Therefore, I can't recommend them because it never happened. Your local doctor is my best advice.

What is ED?

Per the Mayo Clinic (1) yes, I'm going to cite a professional medical organization to stay out of trouble: "Erectile dysfunction is the inability to get and keep an erection firm enough for sex." I think we all get the concept and know the end results or lack of results from ED. Although testosterone will help with erectile dysfunction issues, it's not the silver bullet solution for all men. Therefore, we need to address some of the other products on the market to assist.

Unfortunately, erectile dysfunction is an issue in the bedroom; an experience that 52 percent of men have dealt with at some point or another. When we hit our forties, our testosterone starts to decrease, and we begin to have our issues. Not all men with low testosterone have ED, but there are variables I'll discuss that lead to ED.

Don't be embarrassed about it; one in ten men have ED issues, and the United States has the highest rate at 22 percent of men. After we hit our fifties, about 50 percent of men have issues. I know how difficult it can be if we do have erectile dysfunction issues, especially if our partner is not supportive. If we are unfortunate enough to have an unsupportive partner, the issue only gets worse and the relationship starts to crumble. Going on the premise we are going to take care of it ourselves and not involve our partners, let's address ED.

An issue in the bedroom is obviously the greatest problem we have with erectile dysfunction. Being single now, if we have issues, it makes us not want to date or be intimate. We are afraid of failure, of things not working. This decreases our self-confidence and our social life. It is a difficult cycle; we want to date and find someone, but we are afraid to be intimate with them. This making them feel as if we are rejecting them and then they reject us because there isn't a true connection. Being honest with a new relationship is difficult as well; it's a subject we don't tend to talk about with our doctors, let alone with a new love interest.

As mentioned, we can start with a testosterone test at our doctor's office to see what our levels are. If they are low, deal with a little-bitty needle and get that under control and back up to desirable levels. If we have heart problems, prostate issues, or other medical issues, we might not be able to use testosterone because it will exasperate our conditions.

That is the second step to figuring out our erectile difficulties: visit our doctor, get a physical, and see if we have any underlying issues, such as heart disease or diabetes. These will contribute to ED and we most likely cannot do the testosterone if we have to take medication for these conditions.

Michael Greger, MD, in his book *How Not to Die,* states that ED stands for early death. Not getting an erection is our body telling us there is a problem. A problem with our blood flow through our body. The penile arteries are much smaller than the heart arteries. If the arteries in our penis are blocked from an unhealthy diet, it is alerting us to larger problems in the near future. Again, visit our doctor for a physical.

Getting an erection is more than looking at a good-looking girl and getting excited. It requires our brain, emotions, desires, nerves, muscles, and blood vessels all to work together. An issue with any one of them can create an issue for us. Physical and psychological issues are a problem as well. When I had issues, my doctor said they were psychosomatic because my equipment worked fine; it was just an issue when I was with my wife.

Being emasculated and called names, having high expectations, arguing, fighting, and complaining all of the time just shuts us down. Then, once we have a problem, as mentioned, we start questioning ourselves, wondering if we will be able to perform or if we will disappoint our partner. This might make her complain and start the emasculating process again; it becomes a snowball effect. If this is our issue, getting away from that negative environment might be a big boost to our self-esteem and body functions.

Knowing that our condition can result in a spiraling, snowball effect creates stress for us and our relationship. We can understand that stress adds to ED; it exacerbates our condition. Can we achieve and maintain an erection when we are alone? If yes, then our equipment works. There are other issues at play; most likely those in the last few paragraphs. This can lead to seeing a counselor, a marriage counselor, or a lawyer.

We don't need to be in a relationship where we are being put down due to our issues. If we do not have a supportive partner, it's time to move on. And for those reading this book, we most likely have moved on, so good for our choices. I had great sex immediately after my divorce. My equipment worked fine. I just had some stress and psychological issues based on the marriage.

I am not blaming my ex for all of that stress and those psychological issues. I'm saying life and marriage created those conditions in my life. As mentioned in this book, we need to take responsibility for our actions and challenges we face. Therefore, it could have been my inability to handle those stressful situations. It could have also been my fault for allowing those stressful situations to enter into my life, into my marriage.

What else can cause erectile dysfunction? There are some items that are common and are an easy fix. An easy fix because it will motivate us to be the man we want to be and to motivate us to have great sex again. It will motivate us to be a physically fit person. Yes, one of the issues is obesity; starting today, lose weight, eat better, and exercise. Make that our main focus in life. Do it not just so we can have a sex life again; do it because being a fit, good-looking, and healthy individual will add to our life. There are some medications and diseases that can create problems for us. Again, talk to our doctor about our conditions.

Good news, bad news: tobacco usage can create ED problems. The solution is to stop smoking and chewing tobacco; we know all of the benefits of doing so. In addition, a benefit will be a better sex life. Excessive alcohol and substance abuse add to the erectile problems. Stop spending money to put toxins in our body. By having a clear body and mind, it will help us have a better sex life.

Sleep disorders also add to erectile dysfunction problems; we know this because when we wake up from a nap or from a good night's sleep, we are good to go. When we are tired, we can't make things happen. Remember as teenagers we'd have sex, roll over, nap for fifteen minutes, and then we were ready to go again. As we age, we might need more than a fifteen-minute nap, but it's the same concept; we need to rest our body and mind.

We have so much going on in our minds; we get stressed and can't focus on intimacy. Sleeping and napping clears our mind, and we are fresh. The items in this section are items we should do even if we don't have erectile problems. Losing weight, sleeping more, eating healthier, exercising, not using tobacco, and cutting back on our alcohol consumption can only benefit us.

Medication

First, see if low testosterone is the problem. If so, treating it will benefit us outside the bedroom as well. As mentioned, by taking testosterone, we will have more energy, weight loss, and muscle gain as our body will be operating properly again.

Second, if our condition is bad enough, we might need to do surgery such as penile implants that will manually make us able to get an erection; there is a pump surgically put inside our body. We physically pump up a device inside us to gain an erection. Evidently, it works. I just don't know personally. Obviously, we want to avoid that scenario if at all possible, so let's look at some other alternatives.

The common medications to help treat erectile dysfunction are Cialis, Viagra, and Levitra. Cialis is popular as it tends to last longer—a few days—whereas Viagra will only last for a few hours. They are all effective; they just have different dynamics to how they work. We can usually get a prescription from our general doctor, so we should talk to him about what will be best for our needs based on our physical condition and health history.

There are the over-the-counter medications; we will find a lot of them, but none are proven or tested by the FDA. I've tried many of them; some work, some don't, and even the ones that have worked might have been a placebo where I thought they worked but I had something else in my system as a backup plan. Buyer beware when someone has a magic pill for us.

L-arginine is a pill for blood flow, which I have found to have a noticeable difference in how Mr. Happy looks. Meaning, he is fuller and livelier and does work on his own. L-arginine is in the vitamin section of drugstores and some grocery stores.

And then there are injections. No, I don't mean the testosterone injections into our thigh; I mean the injections directly into our penis. Say what! Yeah, I know it's awesome! I know most don't think it's awesome; in fact, it's terrifying at first, but once we do it, we will love it.

The injections, as of this writing, will require us to get them from the urologist; our general doctor cannot prescribe it. It comes in a kit where the needle, vial, and plunger are all a one-piece apparatus. There are also some kits where we need to screw the various components together. Not a big deal. I like the one-piece as it's quicker, especially if things are going well with our date. We just need to go to the bathroom to "freshen up." We want to be in the bathroom for the shortest period of time possible. Assembly not required is the quickest!

The single shot kit is small enough to fit in our coat pocket or discreetly conceal in a bag or in a sweater. We can excuse ourselves, go into the bathroom, take down our pants, and sit down. Take a deep breath because it's about to get real. With injection apparatus in hand, we hold our penis in one hand, stretch it out a little bit, wipe it with an included alcohol pad, and insert the very small needle into the side of our penis, making sure we miss the large veins.

Once we have the needle inside our penis, and it's not a big needle, it's not like it's going to poke through the other side. We push down on the plunger and the vial will empty into the penis. We pull the needle out; use the alcohol pad to stop any bleeding and make sure the entry point closes. Discreetly put the apparatus back into the package and put the package back in our coat pocket. Don't leave it in the garbage can. Duh!

In about ten minutes, the penis is not going to be at 100 percent, it will be at 105 percent; it will be bigger and harder than ever before. It's an incredible drug! Here is the problem: it will be like that for two to four hours. Yes, even when we finish, our penis will be at 105 percent! Sounds awesome, but after a while, it does get annoying. Plus how long does sex last? Twenty to thirty minutes max. At least we can easily do a round two—or round three if she's up for it.

This is my favorite remedy for a few reasons. First, for me, it works 100 percent of the time. Second, I have one badass piece of equipment ready to go. Third, it doesn't fail. Even if we finish quickly, we can keep on going. Fourth, we won't finish quickly because there is a bit of a numbing in the penis that will make us last much, much longer. And fifth, the biggest reason is it is badass!

If we can stick a needle in our penis, we can do just about anything. Think about it. What kind of man can stick a needle in his penis? We have to be a really tough guy to do it. It doesn't actually hurt; it's mental, we think it hurts, but it doesn't. The results are worth the little pinch that we do get.

Erectile dysfunction is a real issue; it's something we need to deal with. Yes, it's embarrassing to talk about, even to a doctor, but the end result is worth being a little uncomfortable having a conversation with someone. If our partner finds out or knows we use medications or other means to get an erection, does she want to have sex? If so, we need to take a little blue pill or use an ejection, whatever the case, it's a yes or no.

Some women think it's a reflection of them. They don't understand why they don't turn us on. That unfortunately is ignorance or ego; it has nothing to do with them. It's a medical condition that we need to deal with. And the worst part is if we are taking medication and our partner knows, they believe it should just work automatically. Even with Viagra or Cialis, there still needs to be stimulation, romance, and connection for things to work; it's not automatic. Yeah, they still need to do stuff. They can't just lie there.

If we have a partner who is not understanding or willing to work with us on this medical condition, she might not be the right person. There are plenty of things we have to deal with and put up with when dating women. If we can deal with their issues, they should be able to deal with ours.

CHAPTER 9

Goals

> Ever more people today have the means to
> live, but no meaning to live for.
> —Viktor E. Frankl

Goals. What goals did we have premarriage/relationship? Let's revisit them and talk about how to reset those goals and start working on them. It's not too late. It is a better time to pursue our goals; we have experience, wisdom, and clarity to know what we want in life. We now have the skills to help us accomplish them better than before we got married. Now is the best time in our life to set some goals.

I know some are thinking, *Goals? I have alimony, child support. She got the house and bank accounts. I only see my kids every other weekend. I can't think about goals!* Those individuals, more than anyone, need to set some goals; make all of those issues a goal to overcome and handle. It won't be easy; if it were easy, we would all be living in harmony.

If we haven't set goals and gone after them in a while, there are some changes to getting clarity and having the ability to work toward them. We will address these techniques throughout this chapter. The concepts, however, are the same: have some goals, write them down, work toward them, and when things go offtrack, adjust and continue the journey.

There are times when we get close to achieving our goals, but we seem to be missing an ingredient in the process. The Japanese have a philosophy called *kaizen*. This means incremental improvements. Instead of looking at the big picture, look at the small things in front of us right now. Baby steps. Don't be scared of the big item. What is the first step or the next step we can take? Follow through with the smallest actions.

In life, we don't always get what we want, but we do achieve what we must. If we need a new set of tires, we get them; if we need a new washing machine, we get it; if we need a new job, we get one. We can achieve what we must; we are actually experts at it. We need to capitalize on our musts and realize we are resourceful and capable of accomplishing and getting what we must have. In that same vain, turn our wants into musts, and we reach those goals. Whatever we want, if we make it a must, we will find a way.

If we think of that big goal in the visual term of a big circle, it can seem an overwhelming goal to accomplish. If, however, we draw rings in the circle like a dartboard, start from the smallest circle in the middle and say, "What do I need to do today or what can I do today to take me closer toward the goal?" this small circle should be easy and doable. The next circle will be what we can do in a few days or a week; the next circle should be what can be accomplished in a month. Eventually, that circle will be filled in by smaller accomplishments, and eventually the circle doesn't look that big and intimidating.

If we keep doing what we are doing, where will we be in one or five years? One or five years will be here regardless. Are we going to be the same or living far beyond what we can even imagine now? That is where I am at; over the past several years, my life is far beyond where I could have imagined it. Now thinking ahead one to three years, I can see where I will be based on my trajectory and will be living a life I never expected to.

One way to accomplish goals and live a life we can't imagine is to start by making new friends. That comes from chapter two of this book, "Making New Friends." It is the friends I've attracted into my life who have built up my self-esteem, encouraged, and supported me. It is that circle of friends who has taught me new experiences and skill sets, and through learning new things, I have opened up new goals and dreams. Goals and dreams that I never thought I would want or would want to accomplish.

Stepping outside my comfort zone has made me realize there is more to life—more possibilities than the route I was on. We all have blinders on based on our life experiences; we think we know all there is to know about how our life is and where it should be. We think we know what is possible at this juncture.

Where I am in my life is not anywhere. I could have written a script about five years ago. Five years ago, the things I'm doing now weren't on my radar—not even an interest. That wasn't from goal setting; it's from life experiences. It is from meeting new people who have opened my eyes.

With these new experiences, I have made new goals and can see how they are achievable because I have a support group of like-minded people. We can allow our destiny to materialize organically from doing different things and trying different experiences. Goals are important, but with our new life as a single individual, we need to make new connections, and having new experiences will allow us to have a new vision.

Zig Ziglar said, "You can get anything you want in life, if you just help enough other people get what they want." Most happiness comes from being in service to others, a cause, or a company. That has become my journey; being a part of Toastmasters has put me in service to others. Public speaking is one of the biggest fears of most humans, and to welcome, comfort, and encourage a guest or new member to the club is a great responsibility I have. It's not a responsibility other than I am the current president of the club; it's more of a privilege to be a part of their public-speaking journey.

This service to others has changed my vision as to what I am capable of; it is now about how I can help others. Not only am I currently the president of my Toastmasters Club, but I also just became an area director overseeing four clubs. I am able to help even more people and clubs overcome their fears. Now I have the mindset of going further in Toastmasters, helping more people.

And of course, this book and the programs I will create to help divorced men rebuild their lives and start over—to help them start an even better life. Service to others is a wonderful thing; it brings joy into our life. Service to others at Toastmasters has made me expand my life coaching practice to include public speaking; I coach individuals to become more polished and competent speakers. It is these new experiences that open our minds and opportunities.

In her book *The Secret,* Rhonda Byrne's premises is whatever we want to attract into our life, just put it out into the universe and it will come to us. If we believe it, really desire it, and ask the universe for guidance, we will obtain what we want. If we have read her books or watched the movie or videos, we might have become frustrated when those things we put out into the universe did not materialize in our life.

Recently, I did see a documentary, a follow-up to the initial book/movie that had some clarification. *Beyond the Secret: The Awakening* said yes, we need to put our desires out into the universe for them to materialize, but we also need to do the hard work to make things happen. We can't just sit on our hands, ask the universe to provide for us, and do nothing. I agree with this premise: whatever we put out into the universe, we will receive an answer, guidance, opportunities, or direction. This has happened to me again and again, but we need to do the prep work before it happens. Once it does happen, we need to do the hard work to make it become a reality. Work is always a part of getting what we want in life.

Here is my example and perspective. After being in Toastmasters for just over two years, my life coach gave me a bold challenge. She said, "In the next thirty days, get a paid speaking job." I said, "What? That's nonsense! Yes, I'm with Toastmasters, but I'm not a good public speaker, not even an average speaker. I am a person who is now comfortable standing up and giving a speech or presentation. But I'm not a polished speaker. No one is going to hire me." She heard my reasons and said, "Oh, OK, so thirty days, paid speaking gig."

I pay her money, and I want to get my money's worth; therefore, I realized I had to get a paid speaking gig in thirty days. That's the thing about coaches. They hold us accountable, follow up, and see if we have followed through. Reluctantly, I put it out into the universe, and by that, I mean I thought about it, and I spoke about it out loud—mostly talking out loud about how silly of a request this was and it wasn't going to happen. Nevertheless, it was out there.

Now I have done the hard work to be comfortable standing up in front of others while speaking. I have had some bad experiences speaking, but I've continued to practice and work on my craft. I know that I can stand up in front of a crowd and talk; it's doable. That is part one of the process: build the foundation, and have the skill set to do what we want to do by acquiring skills, education, or practice.

Part two was to put it out into the universe and see what answers come back to us. What opportunities can we see? I had never thought of being a paid public speaker; it wasn't in my vision. Maybe in a few years when I can be articulate and command a crowd like Tony Robbins, but definitely not now. But there it was: the challenge to get a paid speaking gig. I could do it. I just knew no one would hire this rookie.

A friend owns a business called Get Me Some Green, a CBD store with other goodies. On Friday nights, she has free live music; she will have a sole performer play music and sing for about three hours. I've gone a number of times to support her and enjoy the music. The universe spoke to me, an opportunity appeared. I said to Heather, "Do you think next time I could introduce the performer as the master of ceremony?" She said yes! I then said, "But I'd need you to pay me $1 so I can become a paid, professional speaker." She again agreed. I did it! I actually did it. I was booked for a paid speaking gig.

There are those who might be giggling at something so silly and simple, but it's a start. It is momentum; it is the first step along my public speaking journey. I got paid $5 actually; I think it was because she didn't have a single on her, but a $5 speaking gig within thirty days—I did it. That was the third step; prepare, put it out into the universe, and then act on the opportunity when it appears. The point is what do we want to do in life—later in life? Why not try it now? Maybe a small opportunity will come our way and we can see it actually happening and becoming a part of our life.

I've heard a number of people say, "We do not take action because of fear of failure." I would disagree with that. I believe we do not act because we are afraid of success. Success is change; we will have to make changes in our lives to accommodate success. We might have to move to a new city for an opportunity, become a leader, which we are not prepared to do, and might have to be a public speaker! Success is actually scarier than failure.

We are all good at failure; we've done it time and time again. Failure is not scarry; we can handle it. If the phone gets turned off, we know what to do: scrounge around, find some money, and go to the local phone company or check cashing store to pay the bill. As I previously mentioned, it took me a year to hire my life coach; I knew once I hired her, my life was going to change for the better. I'd have to challenge myself, step outside my comfort zone, and succeed. If we acknowledge this truth, we can then conclude our goals are attainable. What is it in those goals that we can successfully accomplish that scares us? Maybe our goals are not in alignment with what we want out of life.

One of the best pieces of advice that I've received about goal setting is to work backward. What is our goal? What does our life look like when we reach that goal? A few months prior to reaching our goal, what actions did we need to take in order to accomplish it? What were we doing six months before that? What steps were we taking to get us there? A few months before that, what challenges came up? How did we overcome them and continue? Work backward. What were all of the steps we did to get there?

When we make that road map, we know the journey we need to take with the anticipation of all the obstacles we may face and how to overcome them. I like to reengineer things; this is a great tool to help us with our goals. Many times, we struggle trying to figure out how to get started; what is the next step in the process, and how can we possibly accomplish a goal? Working backward gives us the assumption we can and will reach what we want. We then work backward to see what we did to get there.

If we want to go old school, following are steps to set and accomplish our goals.

First, know the why behind our goal; why do we want to achieve it in our life? What will it bring to us emotionally? How will we feel having this goal, accomplishment, or achievement? Imagine ourselves already having it. What are we feeling? Who is with us? Are our loved ones, family, friends, or others with us? Or will this alienate us? Just because we accomplished something doesn't mean we can share it; others still need to work and handle their life.

We need to make sure this goal is for us; we don't need to rely on others to bring us joy once we acquire it; we need it for our own reasons. For instance, if our goal is to have a nice condo in the Caribbean, we might be hanging out there alone. Everyone else is busy. They can't get the time off and can't afford the airfare. If we want a condo in the Caribbean so we can have solitude, focus on writing a book or creating a plan for a new business venture, then we have our answer.

If we want to buy an awesome new vehicle to impress our friends, can we save a few hundred thousand dollars by working at a nonprofit? By starting a nonprofit or being a person they look up to? Decide on our outcome and see how we might be able to accomplish it with different goals.

Second, write our goals, study our goals, and/or do an Excel sheet on how to accomplish what we want to. At this point in time, my major goal is to quit my job and hike the Appalachian Trail for three to four months. Hiking the AT is 2,190 miles from Georgia to Maine. There is something inside me that says to do it. I'll have to quit my job as they do not allow unpaid leave.

I've made an Excel sheet with all of the expenses I will have for four months. I won't have rent, electric, gas, water, etc. bills. Once I put it on paper, I saw it was doable. Being able to figure out my annual bonus, which I would be eligible for if I work until December 31, as well as PTO I can use, I'd still have income while I'm hiking the trail. Financially, I was able to do it.

Then I had to do another Excel sheet for what I needed to pay off: my debit that I wanted to reduce so I would have lower expenses during the hike. Finally, page three of the Excel document was the money I would need. The food, the equipment, travel to get home, emergencies, hostels or hotels, new boots (need about three pairs to hike that long), and related items. Food actually became the largest expense; good-quality food for hiking is expensive. I look at that Excel documents every few days; I analyze it and see where I can make changes. I look at other options for food. It is on my mind daily.

By documenting our goal and all that will go into it, our mind is focused on it and answers will be provided to us. Writing our goals down one time is not enough; we have to review and revise them regularly.

Third, check our status, know our progress, and determine if what we are doing is working. Are we getting closer to our goal or farther away? As mentioned above, I'm always analyzing my trip, including how long it will take, how fast I must go, and how many miles a day I must hike. As I research hiking the trail as well as doing training, I discover different things about the hike. I go in and make those adjustment on my Excel sheets and overall plans.

For instance, I am going to push to complete the hike in three months, starting at the end of February and hiking twenty-five miles a day. What I did not factor in was daylight saving time: March–April. It gets dark sooner, so I won't be able to hike until seven or eight o'clock at night. During that time in the mountains, I can get one to three feet of snow; my goal is to have a pace of three miles per hour, but I can't do that in several feet of snow. I've had to recalculate and figure out how to bank some miles with the anticipation of having to do maybe two miles per hour at best.

If our goal is important to us, focus and think about it all the time. Research, analyze, practice, and determine how we can make it happen. Change our approach to accomplishing our goal; what substitutes can we use in the process? Changes to our approach will keep us engaged and always thinking of ways to do it.

Fourth, who do we need to help us accomplish our goal? Who is an expert in the field that we are pursuing? Can we befriend them? Can we ask them for information? Can they be our mentor? Think way ahead, toward the end of our goal/journey. Who will we need to know to close the deal? We need to find a way to know them now. Other people are our biggest resource; they can help us achieve things in life more quickly than trying to do it on our own. Why reinvent the wheel?

I've watched just about every review on YouTube about camping equipment such as tents. I've analyzed every pro and con, the costs, the weights, the durability, and what my preferences are. It can take me days to pick a mug for my morning coffee. I leave no stone unturned when I'm looking for the best item to accompany me for three months in the wilderness. I receive advice from everyone, listen to their reasons, and in the end, make my own determination. But what I did not do is just buy the most expensive, lightest piece of equipment.

Sometimes we think that we have tried to reach a goal that we really wanted in the past, but we can't make it happen! We need to be honest with ourselves. Have we tried everything, or have we tried one or two things that didn't work out perfectly so we gave up? If we haven't tried everything, chances are it is not a real desire; it's a dream, a pie in the sky. It's a lottery dream; if we win the lottery, then we will have this particular lifestyle. But we are not willing to do the hard work to accomplish it.

Ask better questions, and reframe.

If we ask ourselves, "Why are we so fat?" our mind will answer, "Because we eat too much junk food." Instead, reframe the question to "How can we lose weight and enjoy the process?" Our mind will get to work and say something like "Get outside, exercise, eat healthier foods, and spend time with like-minded people who do the same activities." I don't know how I'm going to obtain this goal versus how can I obtain that goal. What skills do I need to develop to make this happen? Speak positively to ourselves. Do not add the element of doubt.

Ask a better question, get a better answer. It's something very simple to change in the process of accomplishing goals but something individuals struggle with.

Reframe the meaning or name we provide to something. For instance, if we are trying to quit smoking, instead of saying, "I am not a smoker anymore," say, "I don't smoke." It shuts the conversation down. People won't say, "It must be difficult, do you want to try one for old times' sake?" No, we are not a smoker, we have no interest in the product. It's our identity; we are not a smoker. Some people like to post on Facebook or announce to their friends that it's been six months since their last cigarette. We are not a smoker; it's a nonissue from here on out.

Reframe an action. If we want to lose weight, instead of going on a diet, we try fasting. On a diet, we can cheat, have just one cookie. When we fast, everything is a no, we only drink water. There is no cheating. We either fast or we don't.

When we accept a challenge from others or ourselves, don't say, "I will try it and see." This is not a decision. A decision is something we are committed to. We say, "I will do it." There is nothing more to say. We are going to do it.

The way we talk to ourselves about our goals and desires will get our mind working. Always talk about our goals in the positive; know that we will accomplish them. As long as we do the hard work needed to obtain that goal, we will make it happen. Remember when ideas and solutions come to us, write them down. Once we write them down, our mind is free to start thinking about other ideas or solutions. If we don't write them down, our mind is focused on remembering them. Help the creative process by writing down an idea when we receive it.

CHAPTER 10

Budget

Don't lower our standards; always raise our standards. When the rent is raised or we take on additional financial liabilities, we tend to ask ourselves, "Where can I cut back?" Instead, we need to ask ourselves, "What do I need to do in order to maintain or increase my current lifestyle?" There is always a way, and we always find a way. Several years ago, if someone asked me if I could pay what I'm currently paying for rent and a car payment, I would have said no! Yet here I am, and anyone can and will find a way. We just need to change our mindset and find a way to make it happen.

This is another chapter where I need to say I am not a financial advisor and therefore cannot provide any financial advice. That is not my intent. I am looking to provide the reader with guidance based on my experiences—what I went through as a divorced man trying to figure it out. When in doubt, always consult an accountant or financial advisor.

My ex-wife handled the finances; she paid all of the bills, saved the money, and budgeted the money. In turn, we had nice homes, vehicles, and vacations, the kids went to private schools, and then college. I don't recall the exact amount, but I gave her 90 or 95 percent of my paycheck and she took care of the rest. "Took care of the rest." Yeah, I'm laughing out loud now too!

I can remember a time when a neighbor came over and asked me, for a reference point, how much our electric bill was each month. I didn't know: $50, $100, $300? I had no idea. That wasn't my department. I had to go ask my wife how much it was. I knew what our mortgage was, but I really didn't know how much all of the other bills were, even after asking a number of times. The point is I didn't do the finance; I had no idea how to pay bills. We were married eighteen years, things changed, many things were paid online, bills were out of my focus.

When I became single, I had to figure it out, and unfortunately, I made many dumb mistakes; I blew through so much money and made poor choices. I then made a budget and could visually see what was going on with my financial life. I developed an Excel sheet that showed each paycheck, what my take-home pay was, and then listed each and every bill I had. At the bottom were the end results: income minus expenses equals disposable income. I will share a sample below so we can develop a budget fairly easily.

By creating a budget, we are creating a road map; we will know where we are going. We will know how much we have to spend on nonessentials once everything else has been paid for. I am a visual person; using this Excel spreadsheet method allows me to see exactly what is going on financially. For instance, I group things together such as musts first: rent, electric, gas, water, car payment, car insurance, and such. Then I have another group for nonessentials, and then credit cards. It was the group of credit cards that caught my eye. At one point, I was paying $1,000 a month to keep up with my credit cards as well as paying just a little more on each card.

That visual budget showed and made me realize I needed to handle those credit cards because $1,000 a month was ridiculous. If I was just randomly paying my credit card bills, I might not have seen the patterns and the problems. Having a budget and a list of all our expenditures and income gives us a great understanding about our finances.

Think of a budget like a diet. We know the only way to effectively lose weight is to eat fewer calories than we burn. Same thing with money. We need to spend less than we make. Looking at the numbers. We won't spend what we don't have.

The good thing about having a budget, especially like the one I have on an Excel spreadsheet, is we can forecast down the road. I usually have six months to a year of finances listed out. I can see, for instance, come the holidays, how much money I'll have for gifts. Do I need to start saving for holidays and birthdays, or will there be enough money after bills to take care of those needs?

In addition, I like to look at my budget and see where I can pay things in advance. For instance, the revolving credit I have for my washer and dryer is around $80 a month; on average, I have it paid three months out. I can see the zeros where there should be payments for that debit. Also, there are some pay periods where one pay period I have $10 left over after the bills but the next pay period I have $450 left over. I look for bills that I can pay on the next pay period without penalty so I can have a little some extra cash on both pay periods. The visual budget lets me see this and plan.

Another benefit are vacations; personally, I like to take cruises. If a cruise is $2,500 and I pay the $500 deposit, I might have to pay that $2,000 balance in six months. I can show paying it off as an expenditure on my spreadsheet. I will then have it paid off before the due date or at the due date.

This budget can also help us save and invest money. If each pay period we have $300 left over, we can add a line item for putting money into our stock account or our Robinhood account. It doesn't have to be a lot, but it's more than we might otherwise invest or save. With Robinhood, I like to round up and use that to invest small amounts. For instance, after paying all of the bills, my disposable income might be $323.20. I will take $23.20, put it in my Robinhood account, leaving me a nice $300. If I go to dinner, buy some groceries, then the disposable income might be $205.72; I'll transfer that $5.72 into my investment account. It's easy and adds up over time.

As we can see on my Excel sheet, toward the bottom I have line items for groceries, restaurants, Amazon (I buy a lot from there), and then a few items listed as "Other," but I change that as needed. Again, it's a visual; we can look at the amount we are spending for groceries as well as the amount we spend on restaurants. If we see our restaurant expenditures are more than the groceries, maybe it's time to start eating at home and not spending so much going out.

Finally, with a budget, we will have less stress and sleep better at night. We tend to stay up at night worrying about our finances, but when we have it on paper, it's almost like we've taken care of it. We've addressed it; we can see it. Yep, we are going to be $109 short next period. We don't have to worry about it right now; nothing can be done; our mind doesn't need to retain that information or data trying to figure out what our next paycheck will look like. The information is right there on the Excel sheet. We haven't solved the problem, but it's been addressed and now that it's out of our mind, our mind can start to find solutions.

In a scenario like this, I'll look at which bill or bills can be paid a week or two late (depending on how often we get paid) without penalty or hurting my credit. For instance, I have until the sixth to pay my rent before I get a penalty. Will that six-day grace period allow me to move the payment until the next pay period?

Let's get to my little Excel budget program.

	1-May	15-May	1-Jun	15-Jun	1-Jul	15-Jul	1-Aug	15-Aug	1-Sep	15-Sep
Salary	1500	1500	1500	1500	1500	1500	1500	1500	1500	1500
Rent 5/1	-900		-900		-900		-900		-900	
Internet 5/17		-62		-62		-62		-62		-62
Electric 5/25		-56		-56		-56		-56		-56
Gas 5/13	-22		-22		-22		-22		-22	
Water 5/4	-31		-31		-31		-31		-31	
Rent Insurance 5/10	-17		-17		-17		-17		-17	
Auto Loan 5/16		-300		-300		-300		-300		-300
Auto Insurance 5/28		-209		-209		-209		-209		-209
Balance	530	873	530	873	530	873	530	873	530	873
Carwash memb 5/1	-32.16		-32.16		-32.16		-32.16		-32.16	
NetFlix 5/18		-13.93		-13.93		-13.93		-13.93		-13.93
MLB.TV 5/12	-21.22		-21.22		-21.22		-21.22		-21.22	
Apple Music 5/10	-10.71		-10.71		-10.71		-10.71		-10.71	
Amazon Music 5/24		-4.28		-4.28		-4.28		-4.28		-4.28
Balance	465.91	854.79	465.91	854.79	465.91	854.79	465.91	854.79	465.91	854.79
Barclay CC 5/5	-25		-25		-25		-25		-25	

BOA CC 5/17		-40		-40		-40		-40		-40
Chase CC 5/30		-40		-40		-40		-40		-40
Conns Furniture 5/30	0	-80	0	-80	0	-80	0	-80	0	-80
Balance	440.91	694.79	440.91	694.79	440.91	694.79	440.91	694.79	440.91	694.79
Ally Invest		-50		-50		-50		-50		-50
Robinhood	-25		-25		-25		-25		-25	
Balance	415.91	644.79	415.91	644.79	415.91	644.79	415.91	644.79	415.91	644.79
Grocery Store	-98.73	-156.42	-75.88	-88.98	-103.91	-105.57	-72.66	-116.31	-74.01	-98.4
Restaurant	-54.55	-49.22	-98.55	-72.05	-51.39	-175.2	-39.51	-78.09	-28.72	-86.66
Amazon	-37.52	-40.6		-106.77				-119.7		-24.12
Other										
ATM, cash-tips	-40									
Apple, ebook	-16.08									
Balance	169.03	398.55	241.48	376.99	260.61	364.02	303.74	330.69	313.18	435.61

Bills, bills, bills.

At the top of the Excel sheet, I have each pay date; obviously we would put our exact pay dates, as we know when we're getting paid. Under that, I have my take-home pay, what actually gets deposited into my checking account. I have the income line as salary; if we have a part-time job or a side hustle, we could add some line items for each of those. Or if we have a roommate, that would be income when they pay us. Notice the salary and/or any income items are a positive where all of the expenditures are a negative. Double-check on a regular basis because I have accidently put in a bill and showed it as a positive that threw off my actual spendable amount.

The salary, or income amount, is not only after tax and deductions of health insurance, 401(k), and such; it is also the amount that only goes into our checking account. For instance, I have part of my paycheck go into my savings account and then the balance into my checking account. Therefore, I have already invested money into my 401(k) and put money into savings through direct deposit. Then what is deposited into my checking account is what I have to spend on bills.

I then start deducting my necessities: rent, internet, electric, gas, water, renter's insurance, auto loan, and auto insurance. Based on the due date, I know which pay period I need to deduct from. For instance, rent is due on the first of the month; therefore, it's paid from that pay period. I have a grace period where I can pay up to the sixth without penalty. Most likely our paycheck will not always be on the same date of the month. We might get paid every other Friday; however, it won't be on the first and fifteenth. If we get paid on the first and fifteenth, it makes things a little easier for us to plan. If our dates are sporadic, we'll need to make sure we put the deduction in the right pay period. I do a subtotal after that section. On the Excel above, on May 1 paycheck, my subtotal is $530 after paying rent and other necessities.

My next section is nonessentials—items I could get rid of if I was in a pinch or needed to reduce my bills. They are items I enjoy and want to make sure I don't have to get rid of them. These items are $82.30 a month, including my monthly car wash membership that I use several times a week, my Netflix account, MLB.TV package for my phone/computer, Apple music for my phone, and Amazon music for my Alexa. These are all simple pleasures, just not necessities. Still on May 1, after I paid my necessities, and then my nonessentials, my balance of spendable income is $465.91.

On to the credit cards, in this section, I show the minimum amount due. I never pay the minimum amount due, but that's what I show on my Excel sheet. That way I know where I'm at financially and then I adjust the payments based on how much is left over. For the Barclay credit card, my minimum payment due is $25; it would be OK to pay just that if I was running a little short; however, I would rather pay a little more or pay it all off it possible. I like round numbers, so if my credit card balance is $242.17, instead of paying the minimum of $25, I would pay $42.17. That's just me. Obviously, I'd go into the Excel sheet and change that number from -25 to -42.17 so it balances properly.

Any amounts we change, we will manually go in and make the adjustment; it needs to be precise. My electric bill on May 15 is shown as $56; that is just a close estimate. I will need to change that number to the exact amount once the bill comes in. That is where the Excel sheet helps; we can forecast what variable bills will most likely be month after month. Following the flow, after my necessities, nonessentials, and credit cards, on May 1, I am now at $440.91.

Next up, my outside investments such as my Ally Investment account, where I buy my stocks, and Robinhood, where I buy cryptocurrency and some stocks that I will do day trading with. Since I have a 401(k), pension and saving that are automatically funded from my paycheck, I don't need to put money into them. Again, like the credit cards, I just put a minimum amount I want to invest each pay period, but it is usually more. Depending on how much is left over and what the market is doing, I might put much more or just the minimum. For simplicity, I have only shown the Ally and Robinhood; however, we may have more line items for other investment platforms. Now under May 1, I am at $415.91 left over.

Finally come the items that change all of the time and we need to make sure we are putting the right amounts in there, which I'll talk about in a moment. Groceries are always changing; restaurants, including fast food, are always changing. Amazon has become a line item for me since I order so much from it. Then I'll have a number of line items called "Other" that are changed all the time too. We can see one says "ATM"; this was for cash so I could tip the kennel where my dog was while I was on vacation. Then I bought an e-book from Apple so it would be on my phone.

For each pay period, I am always changing the line items in this section so I can keep track of them. I just like the reference so I can go back and make sure I deducted everything I spent money on. The last item says "Apple, e-book"; however, I might have five items in that cell saying something like "Apple/Stamps/lottery/haircut" and such. That way, I can see where I am deducting the Apple e-book, my stamps from the post office, my online lottery, and my haircut including tip.

We can't see all of those items on the cell until you hover over it, but they are there for a reference. After deducting everything, I have $169.03 left over on May 1. This is where I will decide to add a little more to my credit card payments, a little more to my Robinhood account, etc. This is our disposable income. I also cross-reference on a regular basis to my checking account to make sure I haven't forgotten to add some deductions.

For the cells, as mentioned above, I might have the "Apple/Stamps/lottery/haircut" in the one cell to the left. In the cell where it says "-16.08" right now, that number would change because that $16.08 is only for that e-book. As I buy things such as stamps from the post office, I will add it to the first cell then I will add the amount to the cell to be deducted. The -16.08 cell would then look like the following formula: $=-(16.08+9.50+20+24)$. The cell would then show -69.58 ($16.08 for the e-book, $9.50 for stamps, $20 for online lottery, and then $24 for haircut including tip). I list every item I spend money on; otherwise, it won't be in balance.

Many of my cells have that same formula in them: $=-(1+1+1+1)$. I don't want to miss an item. Plus, for instance, Robinhood, I might invest the $25 but then decide the market is right and I have that extra $169.03 available and will put more into it. Liking round numbers, I would probably add $19.03 so my available spending money is now $150. In that cell, which shows -25 for Robinhood, I would change it to $=-(25+19.03)$, which would show -44.03. I might have a number of items in that formula as I get anxious and throw another $10 in to buy Doge.

On May 15 when I get paid again, whatever is left over from the previous week I will add to my salary. The May 15 formula would look like $=1500+169.03$ for a positive amount of $1,669.03. Notice I didn't use the negative and then parentheses to make it into a deduction as this is an addition. Usually, I won't bring money over though. I will take that $169.03 and, since I have extra money the next pay period, spend it paying off credit cards or buying more junk on Amazon. On May 15 when I get paid, I will right click on May 1 and hide it so the data is there but now I'm looking at a new period. On that last section, I will put "Other" where "ATM" is and "Apple" is as I will need to add different items during that pay period as they come up.

That's what I do, and I look at this spreadsheet almost daily. As I pay those items, such as rent and credit cards, I will highlight those cells in yellow; that way I know they have been paid and cleared in my checking account. On May 1, I show MLB.TV as -21.22; however, the due date is not until May 12 so I'll wait until it hits my checking account before I highlight it yellow. This way, I know what has been paid and cleared in my checking account, what needs to be paid, and then my checking account should be in balance with my balance on the Excel sheet.

I also color code some cells. For instance, my renter's insurance, auto loan, Netflix, and such are paid automatically from my checking account on the due date. I would highlight these items blue so I know I don't need to do anything.

I still need to go in and manually pay some bills; those would be in the white cells, and once I pay them, I would highlight them yellow. Some items, such as my Apple Music and car wash membership, are paid on one of my credit cards; I then highlight those items in green. For Apple Music and car wash, that total is $42.87. I then pay that $42.87 to my credit card so the balance is available for those transactions. If I have a zero balance on my credit card, once those items are posted, I will go in and pay the $42.87 off.

I am constantly analyzing my finances; I am looking where I could move things around or pay off items quicker. With this example, I have money left over each pay period; in reality, that's not always the case. Some pay periods I might have $500, and the next pay period -$300 left over. What I do is have another line item where I will move $350 from the one pay period into my savings. That leaves me $150 for that pay period. It is shown as -350 on the new line item.

The next pay period, on the same line, I show 350 as an addition because I know I am pulling it from my savings account; it's not salary or income. Now I'll only have $50 left over that period because I'm putting the $350 from my savings into a period where it's -$300, but that's life! Point is we have to get creative and make sure we are balancing and not spending more than we have coming in; this is a great tool to visually see what's going on with our financial world.

Credit

As we know, on the Excel sheet, we can do another tab/sheet. That is where I keep all of my debit and do a debit to credit ratio; that way, I know where my credit card balances are and how they are affecting my credit score. I look at these sheets regularly; if I have an extra $20 to $30, I look and see where I can pay something down. Following is a sample.

CREDIT	Balance	Limit	Usage
CRAP CARD	1,000.00	3,000.00	33%
BARCLAY	-	1,000.00	0%
MASON EASY PAY	235.00	750.00	31%
COUNTRY DOOR	160.00	800.00	20%
CRAP CARD 2	-	1,000.00	0%
CRAP CARD 3	-	1,000.00	0%
FINGERHUT	700.00	1,600.00	44%
TOTAL	2,095.00	9,150.00	**23%**

The section is my credit cards and credit with companies, such as Mason, Country Door, and Fingerhut. I divide balance by the credit limit to give me my usage amount. On our credit report, this is shown as "Credit Card Utilization." The percentages for the most favorable credit scores go 0–9 percent is the best, and then 10–29 percent, 30–49 percent is in the middle, average. After that, 50–74 percent and 75 percent-plus will decrease your score.

Surprisingly, for the first time in a long time, I'm in an OK position; I'm constantly paying down items to get them first to 49 percent and then working toward that 10–29 percent. I'm always scared they will cancel the credit if I don't use it so on the ones with zero balance, I'll put my monthly *Harvard Review* subscription of around $15. Another I have is my Ring Security

Camera subscription of $7 a month. I pay them off once those items are posted.

Obviously, I'm not giving, nor can I give you, financial or credit advice. (Can you see me rolling my eyes?) Everything I've said here is based on my personal experience and perspective. Credit has always been an adversary of mine; I never knew what I was doing, and since my wife had excellent credit, in the eight hundreds, she would purchase everything. Therefore, I never learned, nor did I ever care about my credit. One might be wondering how my lack of credit and lack of caring about my credit affected my wife's credit; it didn't. We had no joint accounts—banking or credit; therefore, she had great credit and I had poor credit.

The problem was when we separated, I went and found an apartment, applied, and was denied because my credit was in the high four hundreds or low five hundreds. They weren't having it. I didn't realize that would prevent me from getting an apartment, plus I had no rental history since we had owned homes for more than eighteen years. I found a nice little ranch house that was managed by a property management firm; I had the same issue with the credit, but they were willing to work with me, I had to pay first, last, and security, which came to around $3,000 at the time. That was a tough pill to swallow, but it got me my own place and I became the best tenant ever; I pretty much paid off the owner's mortgage!

That was an eye-opener. My credit sucked, and it was causing me issues. I got my credit report and started paying everything off, even old debts that were write-offs. I wanted to clean my slate. I paid everything on time; in fact, my credit report said I hadn't missed a payment on anything in five years at one point. Then my credit rose up to the high six hundreds, low seven hundreds, which was still not great, but for me, it was awesome! Then the serpent brought the apple; I started getting credit cards with $1,000, $5,000, $8,000 limits. I felt awesome, like a real person! Then I was getting checks mailed for me: personal loans, unsecured, $2,500, $5,000, $10,000! I was living large and having a great time.

As mentioned earlier, there came a point where I was paying just about $1,000 a month to keep up with the credit card and personal loan payments. My credit started to go down because my credit to ratio was close to 100 percent; I had to focus and get it under control. It wasn't a sustainable situation, so I got one of those debt reductions firms where they negotiate lower payoffs with the credit card and debt companies and then make payments to them on my behalf.

For this to work, we have to let everything go into default; as mentioned, I hadn't missed a payment on anything for five-plus years. Yet my credit was back down into the five hundreds due to this 100 percent ratio and being overextended. Once I went into default, my credit took a big hit, but the company took over and as of today I have completed the program and everything is paid off. My credit is going back up, and I learned a valuable lesson about credit and controlling our financial urges.

My personal experience is if we have or had bad credit, then we really need to focus on repairing it. Be careful of Eve with that apple behind her back. She'll get us in trouble. Temptation! I had eighteen credit cards and personal loans with around $40,000 in debt, but as mentioned, they are now paid off. Yes, it sucks, but we learn as we go through life. I never had good credit, but when I did, companies were handing me money. Be careful out there. Financial institutions know how to entice us, and then we are drowning in debit. Having good credit and money in savings are the best financial advice I can give, but not professional financial advice. Just my own personal experience.

CHAPTER 11

Career

The meaning of life is to find your gift. The
purpose of life is to give it away.
—Pablo Picasso

How are we doing in life right now? Is it difficult? Are we sad, angry, challenged, helpless, financially taxed, or lonely? What adjectives describe our state of mind? Not only our state of mind but our reality as well—the life we are living in. Is it the reason for reading this book? Are we seeking answers and guidance for change?

Now imagine if we get fired or laid off; we have no job, no insurance, no identity, and no camaraderie with coworkers. This chapter is about focusing on our job. Hopefully it's a great job, but if it's a crappy job, we still need it; we need to focus on it and then outperform everyone else. We're going to talk about work, being our best, and by doing so, we are going to get rid of the outside noise that consists of problems and issues we have. We will be the best person in the company, and in turn, our job security will be one less worry.

Our job, our career is more than making money, it can be our identity. We introduce ourselves and either share or are immediately asked what we do for a living. Our response is our identity; we can talk about our career and our position better than just about anything in our lives. Sometimes I forget my daughter's birthdays, other times I forget how old my grandkids are, but I can tell you everything about my career, my industry, my company, professional organizations, and such. Our jobs identify us based on our education, our skill set, our geographical location, our upbringing, and a number of other variables.

Our daily routine of work can help us focus on a task: completing something, having a win when we do a good job, etc. This focus on our work gives us a brief break from the reality of our personal life. Our current personal life is divorce, separation, breakup, or loss of a spouse. Sitting home alone in pain will not lead to any healing or action on our part; we will fester, and the pain will increase. Going to work changes our mindset; we do our work, and later we can fester and cry, but for eight to ten hours a day, we have our busy work to give us some sense of relief.

Now the one thing we've all hated from time to time becomes our safe place. During our divorce, it becomes the one known in our life. It is the thing we look forward to when we wake up; it's an oddity. If it's going to be our safe place, our personal therapy, then we need to make it a great place to be. Embrace it, and do our best.

Imagine how our life would tumble out of control if we didn't have our job, our income. We need to make it a priority, especially now. If our marriage or relationship failed, work gives us that sense of accomplishment, of not failing, but knowing we are able to do anything despite a failure in a relationship. I know *fail* is a tough word; I read it and thought I should change it.

Referring to my chapter on taking personal responsibility, there are times in our lives when we do fail. Maybe the ending of our relationship was not a failure. If we are a widow, clearly we did not fail. I am trying to emphasize the importance of our work and the distraction it creates for us. A loss is difficult. I'm not implying anyone personally failed, but it is a generalization.

Depending on our work, we will have a sense of contribution to the company and our coworkers. If we are in commission sales, for instance, we can constantly step out of our comfort zone by trying new approaches to making even bigger and better sales. As we succeed, our confidence is regained and our self-esteem pulls us through the difficult times.

We need to find fulfilment in our work; hating our job will be depressing. Is there a thought that our job is dumb or irrelevant? I don't believe there is a company or organization out there who is paying anyone just for the fun of it. If we receive a paycheck, we are a relevant part of the organization. Find our purpose; find the reason we are being paid to contribute to the company. Each day when we wake up and go to work, make it count. We need to be the best at what we do regardless of our position or the value we place on it. Take pride in our work; it is important, even if we don't see it. Someone is counting on us.

We need to have a conversation with our boss about our difficult times; assure them we are now focused on the task at hand. Instead of struggling and stressing about work, let our boss know; if we falter, he or she might go to bat for us since we were vulnerable and honest with him or her. I told my boss when I was going through my divorce, and it turned out he was going through one at the same time. He was on a different path than I was. We didn't connect, but at least he could be sympathetic to what I was dealing with, and I with him.

Honesty and vulnerability are our best options; admit things are difficult and taxing on our emotions. Let them know we will do the best we can day in and day out. Commit to making work our focus, and let our boss know.

Push our personal life aside; work is important at this stage.

We can use work to grow: tuition reimbursement, online training, webinars, anything to grown and gain. My company has hundreds of programs and opportunities. Seminars, training, mentoring—anything one could want. There are so many sources out there for us to learn new skills, such as Udemy, iTunes U, and iTunes Books. A Google search will help us find any skill or interest we may have. While working, continue learning and improving upon ourselves. Being a continual learner is key at work and in life. Be curious. Always learn something new. Plus it helps gives us something to do; it will help us pass the time in lieu of sitting around the house moping.

I've taken Excel and Word training programs to make sure I was better than most at the fundamentals. If there is an issue with a Word document or Excel sheet, I can figure it out; I don't need to call the help desk. In fact, I can help others even though that is not the focus of my work. If we can do certain fundamentals better than most, we are ahead of the game; we will be sought out even though these are basic things everyone should know.

Learning will keep us relevant; we will be up to date on all sorts of technology and information in our industry that others who do not have the curiosity will miss out on. I'm sure we have heard people say, "If you need to figure out how to use our cell phone, ask a teenager." Why not have people ask us? We can become the go-to guy.

Continual learning and being curious are mantras we should have in life. In 2009 when I was laid off, I realized that being curious and completing my education would have been helpful. I wasn't prepared; I didn't have a plan B. Now I have an MBA based on that experience; I do not want to be put in a position of not being able to find or obtain a job.

I've been passed up on jobs due to not having the proper education or qualifications. There are still qualifications I don't have; however, I do have the proper education. I'm not irrelevant in the workforce. And it wasn't an easy checkbox I was able to do; it took years of nights and weekends, sacrificing myself, not going out and playing on weekends with friends. Nothing is easy. It takes time and hard work, but the time will come and go; we might as well do something now.

I don't want to say I'm a bragger, but I do let others know what I'm up to. Everyone knew when I finished my bachelor's and moved onto my MBA. When I finished my MBA, people knew. I made sure of it. It was something I worked hard for and accomplished. When I completed my life coaching certification, I let people know. It might sound like bragging, but it's letting others know my qualifications. I could be in the back of someone's mind who might need someone with my qualifications. I'm just increasing my stock in the life marketplace.

Continually learning might lead us down different paths; one example is this book. I started my PhD in business management; three classes in, it sparked an interest in writing this book. Starting on a dissertation showed me how to research and put my thoughts together; it was a great introduction into writing this book. That unrelated thing provided me with the skills on how to do it.

Our job is a big part of our life. Those with spiritual leaning will disagree, but the reality is we need our jobs to buy all of the things those in the spiritual world want to do. How many times have we heard of people who have become enlightened? They gave up the corporate world, stopped practicing law, or sold their business to do what is important in life. They wanted to downsize and live a minimalist life. They want to sit and meditate and live the life they want. I know many of these people.

And guess what they all have in common from their corporate worlds or businesses they sold? A boatload of money in the bank that gives them options to sit around and Zen out on life. Most of us don't have a ton of money sitting in the bank. We need to work so make work our priority. But make it enjoyable, and be the best we can.

As we gain new skills, education, certifications, and designations, it will be time to look for a promotion. We can look outside work for a job with another company, but it's easier to stay where we are. My current company, where I have been at for almost ten years, affords me almost six weeks of vacation, a pension, and many other perks. Leaving and going to another company will knock me down to two weeks of vacation. We need to factor everything into leaving a company, not just the money. Staying with our current employer, depending on the opportunities available, should be our first focus.

I was fifty-four when my company started a mentoring program; I was one of the first to sign up and was fortunate enough to be partnered with one of the top people in the company. For a year, we would talk once a month for about an hour; he would give me advice and guidance regarding the insurance industry and management. Eventually I applied for a position in the company that I ultimately did not get; however, it was a great learning process. The position was posted on the company's site, so I applied for it. Then I sat back and waited. Once I spoke to my mentor, he asked what I had done since I applied. Nothing. I just applied and was waiting for the job to be handed to me on a silver platter, basically.

He told me I had to start networking, to reach out to others in the department I was applying for. He said to talk to the hiring manager and get some feedback as to what she was looking for. One of the nice things we did was practice my interview process. My mentor would do mock interviews with me; he was a top manager in the company so he knew all of the lame answers people would say in interviews. He wanted me to be more authentic and not have those standard answers.

We practiced the interview, and he was harsh, turning negative statements into positive statements and listening for key words, cliché words. It was a real eye-opener, and he gave me great guidance. I reached out to others who I knew in that department and got information and feedback from them. Although I was not awarded that position, it was a great learning experience; we can't just apply and sit back.

LinkedIn is a great resource; we need to start reaching out to those unknown friends we have connected with and network with them. Make ourselves present on LinkedIn and other social media platforms. Do not use LinkedIn to talk about what we had for dinner. Post about how awesome we are and what we bring to the table, just not the dinner table.

One of the things I learned in the interviewing process was to say, and show, we are a continual learner. We want to emphasize we are inquisitive and want to learn and know more. Especially if we are applying to a new department or company. We need to be curious about the company, department, and position. We need to let the hiring manager know we might not know everything, but they should be convinced we want to learn and know everything we need to know. They don't want someone who will come in and push papers from one side of the desk to the other; they want someone to come in and bring energy and a spark to the department.

It's not easy. In fact, it can be discouraging to try to get a promotion. I applied for a management job recently and once again missed the opportunity. I was discouraged because the hiring manager told me I needed to do a little more to impress her, to show her what I have to offer the department.

Really? I've been in college for six years, I have received my MBA, and I am working on my PhD. I am president elect of the insurance organization that is relevant to my career/department. I am president of my Toastmasters club; I am an area director overseeing four Toastmasters clubs. I was part of the mentoring program with one of the top people in the company giving me advice on leadership and growth in the company. Through tuition reimbursement, my company has spent nearly $30,000 on my education. I was promoted to a senior position several years ago for getting my professional designation. Yet I need to prove myself? Yes, that is my laughter off in the distance.

It was Denzel Washington who said, "If you're not failing, you're not trying." As frustrating as it is, I am trying. I encourage everyone to do the same. Don't sit idle. Eventually things will click. Not getting the promotion or a job means we are trying.

Once we are cruising along in our career, it's time to think about our side hustle. That gig that will bring us additional income might spawn a new career, or we even start our own business.

I never thought I would start my own business, but that is what this book is. "How to do life without the wife" is my registered trademark. It is my brand. Once this book is completed, I will turn it into an on-demand video program. Then a YouTube channel, a podcast, life coaching, seminars, and of course, more books.

Can we see ourselves starting our own business? If we have a good, steady job, it's a great opportunity to ease into something we are passionate about. I have some friends who have encouraged me to quit my job and force myself to be all in with this venture. Not! I get the concept, the motivation of no money, but I'm not that guy. I have been doing this for several years now and when HTDLWTW gets me to a certain income, I might leave the corporate world. Therefore, I'm not recommending we quit our jobs and chase our dreams. We need to take our time, cross our T's and dot our I's, and then make that decision. But again, keep our job for as long as we can!

Yes, I have friends who have quit their jobs, chased their passion, and had a nice lifestyle. However, if we are going through a divorce or recently divorced, we have some obligations. Let's not make hasty decisions. That is why I recommend the side hustle to start exploring those passions. We are dads, ex-husbands, and men; let's do the right things in life.

Being single and free again, are there any thoughts or ideas about starting a business? We need to find what makes us happy, what we are good at. We might not think there is a business in what makes us happy, but chances are there is. I heard an interview with John Travolta who gave a good starting point for us. Again, this is another zillionaire who says, "Don't worry about the money aspect," as he looks at the jets literally parked in his backyard.

I don't recall what he said exactly, but in essence it was this: if we want to be a billionaire, take the money out of the equation. What are we going to do to have enough people give us a billion dollars? We have to create something for the masses to buy; we have to provide an incredible service. The money just won't come to us; we need to be of service to others.

That should be our starting point. What can we do that others will pay us for? What can we build or sell that others will buy? As with the chapter on goal setting, reverse engineer the process. We want to make X amount of money as a side hustle so we can eventually quit our job. What does that look like? What are we doing or selling that people will eventually give us that X amount of money for?

This chapter is about our career, and I encourage everyone to put that first. Maybe becoming an entrepreneur is not something we desire. Nothing is wrong with that! I am very happy with my career and being a corporate guy. I am compensated well and have many perks with my company—except for that lack of promotions thing. If HTDLWTW doesn't work out, I will be a happy camper doing what I'm currently doing. Again, we've got to try.

Find a way to love our job if we don't already do so. A majority of our time is spent at work, so make it a pleasurable experience.

CHAPTER 12

Diet

When I started writing this book, I didn't have this chapter. I was encouraged by others to write a chapter about health and diet, but I didn't have that experience in my life yet. I was still eating junk food and whatever I wanted to consume. This book is about growth, and with this chapter, I have found that growth. I'm not an expert. I'm just a person making better choices with my food. As we are coming near the end of this book, I hope that has been the takeaway. We don't need to be perfect at everything, and we don't need to be an expert. We just need to try things and see what works.

I started this book about not focusing on cliches. With a chapter about food and diet, I do have a cliché that might be relevant. With the advice in this book, treat it like spaghetti; throw it against the wall and see if it sticks. If it does, the pasta is ready. If it doesn't, keep cooking, keep going, keep digging for what we need in life to satisfy our palate.

We've discussed the lawyer issue, so let me qualify this chapter. The following information is designed to inform based on my personal experiences, not provide medical or health advice. We should always consult our doctor when it comes to our personal health or before we start any treatment.

I thought when I got divorced I was going to lose weight, get in shape, and start dating lots of hot girls. That was the fantasy; the reality was I gained weight, had poor eating habits, lack of sleep, low energy, and was not able to attract quality women into my life. Divorce allowed me to be selfish, to do what I wanted. I wasn't going to ask for permission for anything. Therefore, I was able to eat McDonald's on a regular basis, go to Hooters, have bags of candy in the house, get donuts when I wanted, enjoy having double-stuffed Oreos in the fridge, and have ample ice cream in the freezer. As mentioned in a previous chapter, I would go to the gym all of the time, work out, go hiking, and use the treadmill, yet I still gained weight. I would justify all the junk food due to my workout regiments.

There is one simple fact. If we consume more calories than we burn, we will gain weight. To add to the issues, they opened a new Starbucks next to the gym; after a good workout, that vanilla bean crème Frappuccino with four hundred calories just cut what calories I burned in half. Once home, a handful of Oreo cookies put me into the negative and anything I ate, including a healthy dinner, would start putting on the pounds. This was a struggle for most of my life. I would decide to burn more calories with longer workouts and then justify eating a bag of candy. I never got control of my weight and was usually thirty to forty pounds heavier than I should have been.

It was when I decided to hike the Appalachian Trail as a through hiker, 2,180 miles over four months, that I made changes. I started training, hiking five to ten miles a day usually with a backpack on or a training vest with ten to thirty pounds. This became a strenuous workout. I could see a change in my physique and energy and a slight weight loss. I was burning around one thousand calories; throw in a quick workout at home, and I slowly saw the scale producing lower numbers.

A friend recommended a TV app called Gaia that has a wide variety of content, such as self-help, meditation, healthy eating, alien encounters, yoga, and other interesting topics. It was there I found many shows on healthy eating, plant-based eating, juicing, and cleansing. I watched every show and documentary on health they had that in turned changed my perspective and habits. I am a very picky eater. I don't like greens, vegetables, beans, or anything healthy. I'm a meat and potatoes person, no sides of course; however, that has changed.

Once again, I am not a nutritionist, therefore my information is not professional advice. It's just what has worked for me. Changing my eating habits has allowed me to lose thirty pounds this year. Along with eating properly and exercise, I have had to buy new clothes, getting rid of the XL items and now wearing large. I am considering moving to mediums.

I'm not promoting dieting or suggesting we do a diet. I believe a healthier lifestyle will help us obtain our goals and live a healthier and more energetic life. On occasion I do eat junk food and have too many snacks. I consume more adult beverages than I should, but I'm able to because a majority of the time I'm doing the right things, consuming the right foods, and exercising. When talking about diets, motivational speaker Tony Robbins reminds us about the first three letters of *diet*. Yes, they are *die!* Dieting is not a pleasant experience and is a short-term solution.

Juicing. As mentioned, I am a picky eater; therefore, I miss out on a lot of vitamins, nutrition, and beneficial foods. Juicing gives me the ability to consume all of those good things without actually having to each that yucky stuff. I consume on a regular basis items like broccoli, kale, peppers, carrots, cucumbers, celery, ginger, and squash. If it can be juiced, I'll drink it. Throw in some lemon, and it's all doable. No, it's not wonderful; however, it's a means to an end that we can do. I don't look forward to having a vegetable juice, but I do look forward to the benefits.

Juicing is time-consuming, not just from cutting up the fruit and vegetables to fit into the juicer but also the cleanup afterward. Do we know what else is time-consuming? Going to the doctor's office, having surgery, and having dialysis. Missing work or special events with our family because we are too sick or have to be under medical care. If things were easy, everyone would do them. Find a way to juice and realize the effort it takes will be worth it in the long run.

Fruits I can do, especially in the morning. Apple and orange juice, almost daily, freshly squeezed, is a nice treat after coffee. I usually don't do a vegetable smoothy; however, I will do a fruit smoothy that consists of just about any fruit item there is. Midmorning or for breakfast, a fruit smoothie is good by simply blending a bunch of fruits with a coconut water base and a little aloe juice. After a workout, I'll blend up some watermelon with a little coconut water.

The point is to find what works for our individual need. We no longer need to scrunch our nose at foods we don't like. Except beans. I do not like beans, and there is no way to juice or blend them, so they are not on my menu at this time. I have found a product called Huel that is a fully nutritious powder meal made of a bean-based product. Add water, coconut water, or put in a smoothy; the Huel product will give us all of the vitamins, protein, and other nutrition we need. And the taste is not bad, although there are some side effects of a bean-based product, especially when we are not a bean eater. Let's just say there are some odorous effects that are noticeable—so noticeable I'll leave the room!

Another treat I've discovered is tea. I have an afternoon tea almost daily. I have one of those metal kettles that whistle when the water boils. I'll put some local honey and a tea bag in a mug, add the hot water, and enjoy the tea as an afternoon treat. The process of boiling the water, steeping the tea bag in the mug, and stirring the honey until it is absorbed in the water is an activity that breaks up the daily routine.

Red wine over rum is a healthier option, although I do love my rum! I read a story about things the oldest living humans drink; they are water, tea, and red wine. Therefore, I'm hedging my odds and doing the same. I like red wine because you can let it sit; it is best at room temperature so we don't need to worry about keeping in cold. I recently discovered Cabernet Sauvignon, which appeals to my palate more than other red wines. With traditional red, I can usually only have one or two glasses, but I can handle a bottle of Cabernet Sauvignon in a night.

My preference is red wine at a company party or going out in a social setting. For whatever reason, wine doesn't get me tipsy. A bottle might make me smile, but it won't make me goofy. A few rum and Cokes or a mojito will create some issues! Find what works for us as we are all different, but make sure we drink what doesn't make us silly at company or social events. I have enjoyed watching too many coworkers make fools of themselves at company events.

When I read about diet and health, I always want specifics. I want to know what I can eat. Most articles or books are very generic and therefore I really don't know. My guess is because we are all different with different tastes, dietary concerns, and health needs. I'm just going to tell what I consume on a daily basis; it's usually the same items I found to satisfy my needs.

I have to wake up with a cup of coffee with almond cream and no sugar. I don't care about the calories or nutritional value. I just need to have that start my day. Usually it is the little pods, but when I have time, I enjoy doing coffee with a French press; it is a fun activity to make my coffee and not just more time-consuming. Yes, the coffee snobs will say you should always have French press; however, I just don't have the time to do it every day. I pick my battles and my pleasures, and having coffee as soon as possible tends to be a priority for me.

Breakfast consists of a two-egg omelet, usually with bacon, sausage, or turkey bacon/sausage, along with some feta or goat cheese and maybe some freshly diced cayenne peppers. I throw in a little turmeric and freshly ground black pepper. While I'm cooking the bacon or sausage, I make fresh orange and/or apple juice. After I drink the juice, I'm usually onto my second cup of coffee or a morning hot tea.

Why turmeric? First, turmeric is a bright-yellow spice that brightens up the eggs a little bit and is just one of those ingredients most people don't use or put in eggs. I use turmeric several times a day, usually for breakfast and dinner. It is a spice that comes from a root in the ginger family, although it is not spicy like the ginger. Turmeric is common in curries and in mustard. According to the Cleveland Clinic,[7] turmeric can help with improved memory and may also play a role in preventing the development of Alzheimer's disease. It helps fight free radicals by neutralizing them and helps lower the risk of heart disease. It can help fight cancer and depression.

Why black pepper? The black pepper acts as a carrying agent for our body to absorb the turmeric; therefore, we should use them together.

Why feta cheese? It has a different taste than the regular cheese we all tend to eat. For me, it's the flavor and just variety. Feta is made from sheep or goat cheese and is a curd white cheese. Feta is considered one of the oldest cheeses in the world. It has nutrients, such as calcium and protein. Feta is associated mostly with cheese from Greece and therefore becomes one of those far-off, exotic ingredients. Feta can only be made in certain areas of Greece. If we make it at our house, it's not feta.

I need to be in the mood for cayenne peppers, so I don't always include them as an ingredient. I grow cayenne peppers at the house, and due to the abundance, I'm able to freeze them and use them during the winter. I have sinus problems; therefore, the peppers get the system going and I'm able to have clean passages by the time I'm done eating.

For lunch I like to have a Huel protein shake. I make it with water only and drink it at room temperature. It doesn't taste great, but it doesn't taste bad. It is a means to an end. If I don't have the shake, I'll do a salad or maybe soup, depending on the weather/temperature. I only like soup when it's cold outside.

Afternoon tea with honey, as mentioned above, is a change of pace and adds something different to my palate. With the honey, it is sweet, and with it being hot, it is sipped and creates a calming effect as we have to slow down. We can't chug it or not be conscious of what we are doing. We need to be present with our tea and enjoy it slowly.

Why honey? Because it tastes good. Eating honey is like eating sugar. It has minimal amounts of fiber or protein. It does have nutrients, but they are too minimal for us to obtain value from them. Honey does have antioxidants—the darker the honey, the better. It is also supposed to help with cuts and burns, although the benefits come from applying it directly to the wound.

The afternoon might also include a bag of microwave popcorn or a granola bar. Not all granola bars are great, but they are my go-to when I need *something!* It's better than a candy bar or a bowl of ice cream and seems to take care of my cravings.

Why popcorn? According to WebMD[8], it is high in fiber and is an antioxidant. Popcorn is a whole grain that can help reduce the risk of diabetes and heart disease. It helps with weight loss since it is low in calories and has the high fiber content. For me, it fills me up, and I don't find myself snacking after I have some.

Dinner is my favorite meal because I'm actually cooking; I am cutting up ingredients and making things at different times to bring it all together. My nightly meal is basically a jambalaya that consists of meat, vegetables, and rice. I do use rice most of the time, but I'll also use pasta for variety. I use different rice products. Much to one of my Asian friends' dissatisfaction, I call them my "rices" because I use a variety of rice products. White, brown, wild, and yellow. I like all types of rice; therefore, I have something different each night.

I start with a little olive oil in a pan. As it heats up, I put in freshly diced garlic and lemon peel. I then add my favorite items: cumin, ajowan, and fennel seeds. As these ingredients are warming up, I will be cutting up some tomatoes. Once the garlic starts to brown, I will throw the diced-up tomatoes into the pan and stir. I'll put in some balsamic vinegar, turmeric, and ground pepper. As the tomatoes start to get soft, I will put in some rice or pasta that absorbs all of the flavors. Finally, I will throw in my meat, which is usually chicken but sometimes sausage. Tonight it was scallops. I'll put it on a plate and then I have a complete meal.

It probably sounds boring to eat the same thing every night, but like I said, there is variety based on the ingredients. It's a time when I slow down and concentrate on the meal. It's similar to having tea; this is just cooking and focusing on what I am doing.

Why olive oil? Monounsaturated fat helps lower our cholesterol; it is an antioxidant and has some anti-inflammatory qualities. It is high in calories, which is a negative.

Why cumin? It comes in seed or powder; I use both but use the seeds most of the time. Cumin has iron and helps with your digestive system. It is believed to help with weight loss, diabetes, and lowering cholesterol.

Why ajowan? I use the seeds to cook. It is an Indian spice that is common in their food consumption. I have also used it as part of a tea mix to help with digestion. I've read it is supposed to stop graying of our hair. I use it fairly regularly and still have gray hair. It is also an herb that can help with skin issues and arthritis.

Why fennel? They do have a nice flavor for cooking but can also help with heart health and suppress our appetite.

Why tomatoes? Tomatoes are a fruit, and I eat them almost daily. As part of a plant-based diet, they can help reduce the risk of heart problems and cancer. To be specific, tomatoes can help decrease the chances of prostate cancer and lower our risk of stroke.

Why balsamic vinegar? First, I love the flavor; however, the health benefits include lowering our blood sugar, promoting digestion, lowering cholesterol, and lowering acid reflux. With vinegar, we shouldn't need so many Rolaids.

One of my activities is around the spices. I use a number of spices in my cooking, including cumin, fennel seed, fenugreek, flaxseed, coriander, black pepper, and ajowan seed. I have a marble mortar and pestle; I use the seeds of the above spices and crush them by hand to create the powder. It is a relaxing activity, and I have fresh spices to put in my food.

At this point in my life, I am leaning more toward a plant-based diet. I do try to limit my meat products and egg, but I'm not obsessed about it. I still enjoy chicken, steak, and porkchops. I do consciously make better choices. We can do our own research on this one as it's a big subject and I do not have the expertise to try to give ample facts.

The saying is "If God didn't make it, you shouldn't eat it." Easier said than done, but it is a good reference point. If it's a manmade product, it is not as healthy and beneficial for us. When we eat meat or other animal products, we are basically consuming the middleman. What type of diet do the animals we consume have? They all eat grass and plants to be big and healthy.

I encourage everyone to look into a plant-based lifestyle. Read a book, watch a video, or go to www.nutritionfacts.org. Listen to the information provided there, and come to your own conclusion. The founder of nutrition facts is Dr. Michael Greger; he wrote a book I read called *How Not to Die*. In his book, he talks about every different disease that can end our life prematurely. He points out there are various medicines to help prevent, cure, or make these diseases more manageable. The overall theme of the book, however, is living a plant-based diet is a better option. A plant-based diet will prevent us from getting those diseases, help slow them down, and even cure some of them. All of this with fresh fruits and vegetables in lieu of medicines full of chemicals. Do a little research, and come to your own conclusions. It's your life. You do you.

Water: consume lots of water, but we know that already.

No, I did not through hike the Appalachian Trail *yet!* I do have a day job and in order to take three to four months off, I would have to resign. There are no unpaid leaves allowed. I was on the fence for a while, but I really like my company car, health insurance, vacations, and money. One day I will do the hike. Right now is just not the time.

In Closing

I am often asked if, knowing what I know now, I could have saved my marriage. The answer is yes. Without a doubt! However, if I had stayed married the way things were, I would have never become who I am today. I would not have been able to grow, learn, and challenge myself; things would have been status quo. Through my learning experiences, I have come to appreciate my marriage—and my ex.

I've learned to truly love and appreciate my ex as well as our marriage. It was a path in my life, an unexpected path to get divorced and change direction. As a person, I have grown. I can now love others. Other humans who I realize are going through something that I don't know. They are on their own path, and I have to love them and appreciate their process. My processes, early on, I'm sure annoyed a lot of other people.

I hope you have found some things in this book that brought you comfort, understanding, and motivation. Motivation to start something new, to step outside your comfort zone and grow. My grandson tries lots of things, such as different sports and activities, but unfortunately he gets frustrated when he's not an expert after doing it the first time.

Les Brown said to dismantle the belief system that practice makes perfect. Practice makes improvements. With practice, you are looking for new breakthroughs, new insights, or ways to do things. You can always go beyond anything you've ever done. You just need to be patient and consistent.

You're not going to be a great public speaker the first time you try. You're not going to be a great golfer the first time you try. Stepping outside your comfort zone is going to make you try new things. Do them. Just know you will make small improvements each time you do them.

We all need to find our way through life and discover what brings us happiness. I hope this book is a step for you to start in a positive direction.

Thank you for reading.

REFERENCES

Chapter 2: Making New Friends

1   "4 Ways a Breakup or Divorce Can Affect a Couple's Friends. GoodTherapy.org," https://www.goodtherapy.org/blog/4-ways-a-breakup-or-divorce-can-affect-a-couples-friends-0324157.

2   Mandel, L. (2017), "Why We Need Friends, according to a Scientist," TheFader.com, retrieved from https://www.thefader.com/2017/03/08/science-of-friendship.

3   Motivational_Videos_Official, retrieved from https://www.instagram.com/reel/COGnIJMHKwf/?igshid=1v45ce2r1urb8.

4   Whitbourne, S. (2013), "Fifteen Reasons We Need Friends." *Psychology Today,* retrieved from https://www.psychologytoday.com/us/blog/fulfillment-any-age/201303/fifteen-reasons-we-need-friends.

5   Larons, C. (2008), "I Promise Myself," *The Secret.*

6   Cherry, K. (2020), "Things to Do by Yourself," Verywellmind.com, retrieved from https://www.verywellmind.com/the-benefits-of-being-by-yourself-4769939.

Chapter 6: Exercise

Mayo Clinic staff (May 2019), "Exercise: 7 Benefits of Regular Physical Activity," Mayo Clinic, https://www.mayoclinic.org/healthy-lifestyle/fitness/in-depth/exercise/art-20048389.

https://www.rei.com/events, "Classes on Camping, Kayaking, Hiking, Rock Climbing, Paddleboarding, Mountain Biking."

Thomas, N. (2021), "Emotional and Social Benefits of Physical Activity," In Motion O.C., retrieved from https://www.inmotionoc.com/social-benefits-of-exercise/.

Chapter 7: Self-Care

https://www.sleepfoundation.org/physical-health/sex-sleep.

Chapter 8: ED

https://www.mayoclinic.org/diseases-conditions/erectile-dysfunction/symptoms-causes/syc-20355776.

https://nutritionfacts.org/video/survival-of-the-firmest-erectile-dysfunction-and-death/.

https://nutritionfacts.org/video/pistachio-nuts-for-erectile-dysfunction/.

Chapter 12: Diet

7   Hopsecger, Nicole (November 2021), "Cleveland Clinic 7 Healthy Benefits of Turmeric," https://health.clevelandclinic.org/turmeric-health-benefits/.

8   Brennan, Dan (September 2020), "Health Benefits of Popcorn," https://www.webmd.com/food-recipes/health-benefits-popcorn.

ABOUT THE AUTHOR

David Jones, an avid hiker and camper, found his inner peace and vision for writing while exploring the mountains. From the moment he stepped onto the Appalachian Trail, he knew it would become a metaphor for his life. He does his best writing with heavy winds and freezing hail hitting the tent in the middle of the night. When he is not scaling the side of a mountain, you will find him engaged in public speaking, mentoring, and coaching those starting their public speaking journey. He holds an MBA, is a Conch, Miamian, and a Tarheel.

Printed in the United States
by Baker & Taylor Publisher Services